"This is vintage Fretheim: provocative theological reflection combined with a careful reading of the biblical text. What does human suffering say about God? At a time when hard questions lead some to turn away from the Old Testament, Fretheim finds rich resources for probing the depths of the person of God and for rethinking the relationship of the divine to the world."—**M. Daniel Carroll R.**, Denver Seminary

"With characteristic erudition, theological depth, and lively engagement, Terence Fretheim illuminates one of the most perplexing issues of faith: why natural disasters? Fretheim brings together a wide range of biblical texts and ably mines them for their wisdom about God's ways in the world. Such wisdom is critically needed when so much misunderstanding characterizes religious discourse today."—**William P. Brown**, Columbia Theological Seminary

"Throughout history and yet today people have tended to view natural disasters as vengeful 'acts of God.' Fretheim has done us a great service by masterfully exposing how thoroughly this traditional perspective conflicts with a careful reading of the Bible's creation texts. Not all readers will agree with all of Fretheim's proposals, but all will benefit from the fresh perspective he brings to the biblical texts, the unsettling questions he invites us to consider, and the magnificent portrait of a loving, power-sharing, relational God who brings into being a dynamic creation full of beauty and risk."—**Greg Boyd**, Woodland Hills Church, St. Paul, Minnesota

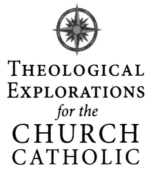

Theological
Explorations
for the
CHURCH
CATHOLIC

Creation
Untamed

The Bible, God,
and Natural Disasters

Terence E. Fretheim

Baker Academic
a division of Baker Publishing Group
Grand Rapids, Michigan

Published by Baker Academic
a division of Baker Publishing Group
P.O. Box 6287, Grand Rapids, MI 49516-6287
www.bakeracademic.com

Printed in the United States of America

Library of Congress Cataloging-in-Publication Data
Fretheim, Terence E.
    Creation untamed : the Bible, God, and natural disasters / Terence E.
Fretheim.
        p.   cm. — (Theological explorations for the Church Catholic)
    Includes bibliographical references and index.
    ISBN 978-0-8010-3893-8 (pbk.)
    1. Natural disasters—Religious aspects—Christianity. 2. Bible. O.T. Job—
Criticism, interpretation, etc. I. Title.
BT161.F74 2010
225.8'36334—dc22   2010010069

10   11   12   13   14   15   16   7   6   5   4   3   2   1

To those who ask why

Contents

Series Preface

Long before Brian McLaren began speaking about a "generous orthodoxy," John Wesley attempted to carry out his ministry and engage in theological conversations with what he called a "catholic spirit." Although he tried to remain "united by the tenderest and closest ties to one particular congregation"[1] (i.e., Anglicanism) all his life, he also made it clear that he was committed to the orthodox Christianity of the ancient creeds, and his library included books from a variety of theological traditions within the church catholic. We at Nazarene Theological Seminary (NTS) remain committed to the theological tradition associated with Wesley but, like Wesley himself, are very conscious of the generous gifts we have received from a variety of theological traditions. One specific place this happens in the ongoing life of our community is in the public lectures funded by the generosity of various donors. It is from those lectures that the contributions to this series arise.

1. John Wesley, *Sermon 39*, "Catholic Spirit," §III.4, in *Bicentennial Edition of the Works of John Wesley* (Nashville: Abingdon, 1985), 2:79–95. We know, however, that his public ties with Anglicanism were at some points in his life anything but tender and close.

The books in this series are expanded forms of public lectures presented at NTS as installments in two ongoing, endowed lectureships: the Earle Lectures on Biblical Literature and the Grider-Winget Lectures in Theology. The Earle Lecture series is named in honor of the first professor of New Testament at NTS, Ralph Earle. Initiated in 1949 with W. F. Albright for the purpose of "stimulating further research in biblical literature," this series has brought outstanding biblical scholars to NTS, including F. F. Bruce, I. Howard Marshall, Walter Brueggemann, and Richard Hays. The Grider-Winget Lecture series is named in honor of J. Kenneth Grider, longtime professor of theology at NTS, and in memory of Dr. Wilfred L. Winget, a student of Dr. Grider and the son of Mabel Fransen Winget, who founded the series. The lectureship was initiated in 1991 with Thomas Langford for the purpose of "bringing outstanding guest theologians to NTS." Presenters for this lectureship have included Theodore Runyon, Donald Bloesch, and Jürgen Moltmann.

The title of this monograph series indicates how we understand its character and purpose. First, even though the lectureships are geared toward biblical literature *and* systematic theology, we believe that the language of "theological explorations" is as appropriate to an engagement with Scripture as it is to an engagement with contemporary systematic theology. Though it is legitimate to approach at least some biblical texts with nontheological questions, we do not believe that doing so is to approach them *as Scripture*. Old and New Testament texts are not inert containers from which to draw theological insights; they are already witnesses to a serious theological engagement with particular historical, social, and political situations. Hence, biblical texts should be approached *on their own terms* through asking theological questions. Our intent, then, is that this series will be characterized by theological explorations from the fields of biblical studies and systematic theology.

Second, the word "explorations" is appropriate since we ask the lecturers to explore the cutting edge of their current interests and thinking. With the obvious time limitations of three public lectures, even their expanded versions will generally result not in long, detailed monographs but rather in shorter, suggestive treatments of a given topic—that is, explorations.

Finally, with the language of "the church catholic," we intend to convey our hope that these volumes should be *pro ecclesia* in the broadest sense—given by lecturers representing a variety of theological traditions for the benefit of the whole church of Jesus Christ. We at NTS have been generously gifted by those who fund these two lectureships. Our hope and prayer is that this series will become a generous gift to the church catholic, one means of equipping the people of God for participation in the *missio Dei*.

Andy Johnson
Lectures Coordinator
Nazarene Theological Seminary
Kansas City, Missouri

Author Preface

These chapters bring together presentations from two lecture series. In October 2008 three lectures were given as the Earle Lectures at Nazarene Theological Seminary, Kansas City, Missouri, under the title "The Old Testament Still Matters." They represent the essence of chapters 1, 4, and 5. In January 2009 the other two chapters on natural disasters were presented during midwinter convocation at Luther Seminary, St. Paul, Minnesota. I hereby thank leaders at both institutions for the invitation to deliver these lectures and for the support given along the way.

Though originally presented as separate lectures, these five chapters address topics that are often brought together in theological reflection and churchly conversation. With the helpful counsel of Jim Kinney of Baker Academic, I have merged them into a single volume, endeavoring to demonstrate how the themes mutually interact. Readers will recognize that these chapters bear the marks of "popular" presentations with a more conversational tone. I hope that these studies will foster further dialogue in thinking both about the texts involved and the basic themes that have been brought forward.

Abbreviations

Old Testament

Gen.	Genesis	Song	Song of Songs
Exod.	Exodus	Isa.	Isaiah
Lev.	Leviticus	Jer.	Jeremiah
Num.	Numbers	Lam.	Lamentations
Deut.	Deuteronomy	Ezek.	Ezekiel
Josh.	Joshua	Dan.	Daniel
Judg.	Judges	Hosea	Hosea
Ruth	Ruth	Joel	Joel
1–2 Sam.	1–2 Samuel	Amos	Amos
1–2 Kings	1–2 Kings	Obad.	Obadiah
1–2 Chron.	1–2 Chronicles	Jon.	Jonah
Ezra	Ezra	Mic.	Micah
Neh.	Nehemiah	Nah.	Nahum
Esther	Esther	Hab.	Habakkuk
Job	Job	Zeph.	Zephaniah
Ps(s).	Psalm(s)	Hag.	Haggai
Prov.	Proverbs	Zech.	Zechariah
Eccles.	Ecclesiastes	Mal.	Malachi

New Testament

Matt.	Matthew		1–2 Thess.	1–2 Thessalonians
Mark	Mark		1–2 Tim.	1–2 Timothy
Luke	Luke		Titus	Titus
John	John		Philem.	Philemon
Acts	Acts		Heb.	Hebrews
Rom.	Romans		James	James
1–2 Cor.	1–2 Corinthians		1–2 Pet.	1–2 Peter
Gal.	Galatians		1–3 John	1–3 John
Eph.	Ephesians		Jude	Jude
Phil.	Philippians		Rev.	Revelation
Col.	Colossians			

Bible Versions

GNT	Good News Translation
KJV	King James Version
NIV	New International Version
NRSV	New Revised Standard Version
RSV	Revised Standard Version
TNIV	Today's New International Version

Introduction

Natural disasters have recently occurred with special intensity in the part of the country where I live, from floods to hail to tornados to droughts. The upper Midwest is not alone. We have participated with millions of others across our country and the globe in a veritable staccato of natural disasters in recent years, from floods in the Pacific Northwest to fires in California, hurricanes such as Katrina and others, earthquakes in China and Haiti, and the tsunamis in Southeast Asia.

And these are only the more-recent experiences. A long history of natural disasters could be cited. One thinks, for example, of the earthquake (and subsequent tsunami) in Lisbon, Portugal, on a Sunday morning in 1755. The churches were full, and many of them collapsed, killing over 50,000 people. And the recent earthquake in Haiti may have killed some 200,000 people. Given this painful history, it is not surprising that the Bible's pages are filled with references to natural disasters and the ill effects visited upon people, animals, and other creatures. One thinks of the stories of the flood, Sodom and Gomorrah, numerous famines, the plagues in Egypt, and even the experience of Job. We often forget that

1

Job's suffering was in significant part occasioned by natural disasters (Job 1). How might reflection on these biblical texts assist our theological consideration of more-recent natural disasters in our world and the associated suffering of both human beings and animals? How might God be involved in such events?

Such theological reflection about God and natural disasters has been on the increase over the last generation or so. Two primary factors seem to be at work. One is the power of the media and technology to bring the effects of such disasters from around the world right into our living rooms and onto our mobile phones day after day. A second factor is the increased environmental consciousness of our time, which has caught up the church and the larger culture in issues relating to the care of creation. Such environmental sensitivity has raised the ante regarding the human role in the development of the natural world. Quite apart from a theological interpretation, many today, both within and without the church, would rightfully claim that such natural events are at least in part due to human activities that have disrupted the delicate balance of the earth's ecosystem. They point to the depletion of the ozone layer, global warming, "unnatural" developments in the animal world (e.g., deformed frogs), the spread of deadly diseases, and weather patterns that seem uncommonly violent. Human beings are often thought to be a problem, if not *the* problem, in the intensity of these natural events, if not their actual occurrence. As we shall see, sinful human behaviors are often linked to the natural disasters reported in the Bible as well.

At the same time, the Bible certainly portrays God as involved in such events. Indeed, from these texts one is given to wonder whether God actually makes floods and plagues worse. For all the talk about God being committed to the care of the earth, in these stories do we not find God contributing to the degradation of the environment!? And if God doesn't take any better care of the environment than would appear to be the case, why should God's followers exhibit any special concern for it? The implications are massive. To put it crassly, if our God cares so much for all creatures, why didn't God create a world in which there would be no natural disasters? We see disease, hunger, pain, loss of life among both people and animals, indeed the extensive extinction of species over the course of the world's history and prehistory (over 90 percent of all existent species have become extinct). Where is God in all of this?

Did God create this kind of world in the first place? One is given to wonder about the nature of God's creation, consistently called "good" in Genesis 1. Can "good" include natural disasters? Most students of this topic would grant that God's good creation was from "the beginning" characterized by "wildness," randomness, risks such as water and the law of gravity, and the potential for ever-new developments in the natural order. Indeed, most would agree that such natural events as earthquakes, volcanoes, floods, destructive weather patterns, cell mutations, and even potentially deadly viruses were an integral part of the creation before human beings showed up. So in some sense, such natural events are God-designed in the very creation of things, and they can be destructive. Much potential for pain and suffering existed in the prehuman, pre-sin world. When human beings did show up, they were told to "subdue the earth" (Gen. 1:28), which must mean that, for all its goodness, God's creation was not believed to be tranquil and perfect. So, in speaking about such matters from a biblical perspective, one must speak of both human and divine factors in the occurrence of natural disasters.

Beyond the issue of creation, isn't God even more deeply involved in such disasters? Some good church people give this theological interpretation of natural disasters: God is in absolute control of these natural events and is aiming these disasters at certain communities, exacting a divine punishment for sins named and unnamed. For example, God aimed

3

Katrina right at New Orleans because of its degradation. Never mind the effect on the children. Although many people are properly reserved in making such theological claims about environmental events, the questions raised are important, not least because many biblical texts link God's judgment on human sin with natural catastrophes. This is true of the major disaster stories we have noted (the flood, Sodom and Gomorrah, the plagues in Egypt) and is apparent in many other texts, for example, this divine word in Jeremiah 4:22–26 in response to human sin:

> "For my people are foolish,
>   they do not know me;
> they are stupid children,
>   they have no understanding.
> They are skilled in doing evil,
>   but do not know how to do good."
> I looked on the earth, and lo, it was waste and void;
>   and to the heavens, and they had no light.
> I looked on the mountains, and lo, they were
>   quaking,
>   and all the hills moved to and fro.
> I looked, and lo, there was no one at all,
>   and all the birds of the air had fled.
> I looked, and lo, the fruitful land was a desert,
>   and all its cities were laid in ruins,
>   before the LORD, before his fierce anger.

And so, given such specific biblical interpretations, are not environmental disasters, at the heart of things, a human problem rather than a divine problem? Indeed, it is commonly thought that such natural disasters occur at all only because of the human fall into sin. At the end of the day, however, such a viewpoint is remarkably anthropocentric. As if to say that stellar explosions are due to human sin! A contrary tradition goes back to the Old Testament, as I hope to show in chapter 1. Moreover, importantly, our increased knowl-

4

edge of the history of nature will not allow us to go there with any confidence. It is quite common now to claim that natural disasters, including pain and suffering experienced by the animal world, were a part of the life of the world before human beings came on the scene. And among the possible interpretations of the oft-cited Romans 8:19–23, God's subjection of the creation to futility is a postfall action and does not speak to the natural order before sin.[1]

The Genesis texts and others do testify that in the wake of human sin there were negative effects upon the natural order, as thorns and thistles complicated the farmer's vocation and the pain of childbirth was "*increased*" (not introduced) for the mother (Gen. 3:16–19). As for the flood, as we shall see, it is directly related to human (and animal) violence in Genesis 6:11–13, which had the effect of corrupting "the *earth*" that God had created. Many later texts could be cited to this effect. Take Hosea 4:1–3:

> Hear the word of the LORD, O people of Israel,
>   for the LORD has an indictment against the inhabitants of the land.
> There is no faithfulness or loyalty,
>   and no knowledge of God in the land.
> Swearing, lying, and murder,
>   and stealing and adultery break out;
>   bloodshed follows bloodshed.
> Therefore the land mourns
>   and all who live in it languish;
> together with the wild animals and the birds of the
>   air,
>   even the fish of the sea are perishing.

And note that God is not named as the one who exacts the judgment; it is the created moral order at work. Acts do have consequences, even cosmic consequences.

1. See, for example, Christopher Southgate, *The Groaning of Creation: God, Evolution, and the Problem of Evil* (Louisville: Westminster John Knox, 2008).

Some observers do want to speak of such events in terms of God's judgment on human sin, and they often do so with energy. But many of us who confess a belief in a living and active God often hesitate to speak in terms of divine judgment, not least because of the heightened rhetoric and undisciplined certainty that often accompany such claims. Other observers do not draw such theological conclusions in the wake of natural disasters because they may recognize our inadequate knowledge of the history of nature and the difficulties of comparing such calamities with one another. Even then, many people, believers and nonbelievers, have been given to a nagging bewilderment regarding such events. Even with such uncertainties, one might ask: Is there not at least a kernel of truth in the linkage of such natural developments to the judgmental activity of God? And if so, how do we draw distinctions? All of this begs the question of what it means to speak of the judgment of God, to which we will turn.

In today's world, then, a distinction would have to be made between moral order in events such as 9/11 (where human sin was clearly a key factor) and cosmic order in events such as the tsunamis—but not an absolute distinction! As we have suggested, moral evil and natural evil do come together in some natural events. Given the interrelated spiderweb of a world in which we live, every creaturely move affects every other creature, for good or for ill. And human sin intensifies the negative effects of this interrelatedness on at least some natural events. Think of Hurricane Katrina, for example, both from the perspective of inadequate human preparations and responses and the possible effects of global warming on the storm's severity—in addition to the social inequities revealed in how the poor and the needy experienced these events at a much more catastrophic level![2] Similar issues have been raised regarding the earthquake in Haiti.

2. For an important study of this neglected issue, see Jon Sobrino, *Where Is God? Earthquake, Terrorism, Barbarity, and Hope* (Maryknoll, NY: Orbis, 2004).

If at least some such natural events can be understood to link moral order and natural order, it is difficult to deny an interpretation of such events at least partially in terms of God's judgment, especially if one defines judgment, as I will, as the effects or consequences of sin. Again, issues of discernment are immediately at hand, and divine judgment needs closer definition. One should not suggest, for example, that floods as such were due to human sin; floods were no doubt characteristic of a pre-sin world. In the Genesis texts, the emphasis is placed not on floods per se, but on the range and intensity of the flood that has been occasioned by human and animal violence.

And so we draw an initial conclusion regarding God's participation in natural disasters: in considering such disasters, we cannot let God off the hook. This is the case from at least two perspectives: on the one hand, such natural disasters are an integral part of God's creational design; God created a world in which natural disasters were integral to the world's becoming, quite apart from human behaviors. On the other hand, specific natural events may be made more severe by human sin, in connection with which one might—indeed, I would say, *must*—speak of divine judgment. In either case, God cannot be removed from some kind of complicity.

At the same time, God is involved in the healing of the environment, so that promises regarding the future of our world can be made: the wolf will dwell with the lamb, and waters shall break forth in the wilderness and streams in the desert (see Isa. 11:1–9; 35:1–10; 65:17–25). And God involves human beings in working toward that goal. What people do counts with respect to the contours of that future. Indeed, their prayers may be caught up by God to help give shape to that hope. And not least because of significant environmental efforts, there are signs of such a positive future all along the way. Such "signs" may be signaled by the work of Jesus. Though Jesus stilled a storm, he didn't remove all storms from the life of the world; though Jesus cured individuals of

7

diseases, he didn't rid the world of those diseases. To use the Gospel of John's "sign" language, Jesus' actions pointed to a future world that signaled the kind of world Isaiah envisioned. Jesus gave signs of a different future that God has in store for the natural world and commissioned his followers to participate with God in moving toward that goal.

A key question: How shall we speak of God's relation to natural disasters and the suffering and death related thereto, both then and now? I don't pretend to have "answers" or "explanations," but some reflections are more helpful than others in sorting out these issues. And they are often more helpful because commonly expressed ideas about God's relationship to disaster and suffering have often hindered the mission of the church. This reality suggests that the way in which we move through a study of the pertinent texts has both theological and practical implications.[3]

---

3. For earlier efforts to work with biblical texts regarding natural disasters, see my essay "The Plagues as Ecological Signs of Historical Disaster," *Journal of Biblical Literature* 110 (1991): 385–96; "Divine Judgment and the Warming of the World: An Old Testament Perspective," in *God, Evil, and Suffering: Essays in Honor of Paul R. Sponheim*, ed. T. Fretheim and C. Thompson (St. Paul: Word & World Supplement, 2000), 21–32.

1

God Created the World Good, Not Perfect

"Community" and "relationship" are "in words" in current theological discussions. All creatures of God together constitute a community in relationship. More particularly, human beings are understood, not as isolated creatures of God, but as part of a global community. Our lives touch the "life" of all other creatures, whether for good or for ill. As Denis Edwards states: "Any contemporary theology of the human . . . will need to situate the human within the community of life. It will need to be a theology of the human-in-relation-to-other-creatures."[1] Everyone and everything is in relationship; reality is relational. Indeed, as we will see, such interrelatedness is true not only of the world of creatures; it is also true of God. Both God and world are constituted by relationships within which one can speak of both commonality and distinction.

1. Denis Edwards, *Ecology at the Heart of Faith* (Maryknoll, NY: Orbis, 2006), 7.

This is a strong biblical claim, though it is not as often recognized as one might think. Even more important, this claim is not commonly interpreted in ways that take relationship language with genuine seriousness.

A negative aspect of this relational perspective is that any damage to the community or communities to which we belong diminishes us all.[2] This earthly home, this community, has been damaged, especially by the actions of human beings. Indeed, the church bears some responsibility, not least by its slowness in recognizing the need, its relatively tepid response (even silence), and all too often its theological perspective. It is remarkably common among Christians that a theology of demolition is in place, wherein it is understood that the world is going to come to an end quite soon anyway, so why bother to be concerned about the needy or the environment.

Another theological matter that aggravates the issue is the common imaging of God. God is often portrayed as a God whose will for the world is irresistible; in the common parlance, "God is in control." This often means that God is one who will "take care of everything," come what may. One implication of such a perspective is that human beings are thereby encouraged to be negligent regarding matters such as care for the environment and let God do whatever God is going to do. Given these realities and other factors, we are faced with a global crisis in which creatures of God's own making are threatened and the home that we share is being ravaged. Jürgen Moltmann puts it this way: "If human beings are themselves 'part of nature,' . . . then any destruction of nature necessarily also includes an element of human self-

---

2. In the use of the language of community and relationships, it is important to remember that communities and relationships can be of many kinds, from healthy and good and loving to abusive and hostile and poisonous. We need careful discernment in sorting out the good relationships from the bad and acting with wisdom. Indeed, the very relational life of God will have to become engaged in order to restore community and relationships to their rightful place in the world. And then the relational life of God must constitute a model for all of us who are created in the image of God, showing us what it means to be in genuine relationship.

destruction."[3] Any damage to the community or communities to which we belong diminishes us all.

At the same time, we can be thankful for the increasing recognition of the issues that are at stake and the remarkable efforts being made to correct, preserve, and enhance our interconnected life together. This "environmental conversion" includes not only Christians, but also people from many different religious and nonreligious perspectives. God the Creator is at work among us all to bring life and healing.

My most basic claim in this chapter is this: God created the world good, not perfect.[4] In support of that claim, I will think closely about the kind of God who is depicted in the creation accounts (Gen. 1–2) and what sorts of creational moves God makes. I will argue that God makes a decision to create in community rather than alone; at the divine initiative, the creation plays an active role in God's creating work. Then I will explore the implications of that divine move for the life of both creature and Creator and, more particularly, for our environmental considerations. I am especially interested here in setting a stage for later chapters on natural disasters.

I will work with the two creation accounts in Genesis as a single witness to creation.[5] Whatever the history of tra-

---

3. Jürgen Moltmann, in his foreword to Sigurd Bergmann, *Creation Set Free: The Spirit as Liberator of Nature*, trans. Douglas Stott (Grand Rapids: Eerdmans, 2005), vii.

4. For an initial statement using this language, see Terence E. Fretheim, *God and World in the Old Testament: A Relational Theology of Creation* (Nashville: Abingdon, 2005), 41, 52. This chapter seeks to bring a somewhat different organization and theological focus to material presented in that book.

5. Literary and historical issues of these chapters have often been discussed. At this point, I suggest that these texts are both typical and atypical. On the one hand, these texts are typical in that they reflect life, especially human life, in every age. At the same time, the past and the present are not simply collapsed into each other. And so, on the other hand, these texts narrate a story of the past; they are concerned to speak about the spatial and temporal beginnings of the world's earliest life. This is the way in which the world got its start. One important virtue of such a perspective is that creation and "fall" are not collapsed into each other, and moral evil is not understood to be a part of God's good creation ("natural evil" is another story, as we will see).

11

dition may have been, Genesis 1 and 2 together constitute Israel's primary witness to the Creator God (and the only nonspeculative one).[6] Many persons have engaged in the study of these chapters, and a growing literature is now available across the theological disciplines. Still, the study of Old Testament resources for this conversation is in its infancy—not least because of the secondary status that creation has had in much biblical reflection.[7] Somehow we must gain a sense that creation is a primary theological vision in the Old Testament and that how we think that matter through will have a considerable effect on related reflections.

Good and Perfect

The most basic statement of Genesis 1–2 regarding created beings is that they are "good" and "very good."[8] *Every creature* is evaluated in these terms; the human being is not given a special evaluative word; indeed, human beings are not even given a separate creation day but rather share the sixth day with the animals. Moreover, this oft-repeated evaluation is reported as a direct *divine* evaluation: *God* saw that it was good; God saw that "everything" was good. This evaluation is *not* reported as an assessment of the narrator, but as God's own evaluation.

What does it mean to be *evaluated* good by God? At the least, it means that God is not done with the creatures once they are brought into being. God experiences what has been created, is affected by what is seen, and passes judgment on

6. For detail, see Fretheim, *God and World*, 29–34.

7. For detail, see ibid., ix–xiv.

8. The one use of the phrase "very good" in the creation accounts occurs in Gen. 1:31, at the conclusion of the sixth day of creation. Some commentators think that the phrase "God saw everything that he had made" refers only to those creatures created on the sixth day (and hence would include both human beings and animals), but it is more likely a reference to all of God's creations up to this point. For an earlier reflection on these matters, see Terence E. Fretheim, "Preaching Creation," *Word & World* 29 (2009): 79–81.

the results. This divine way is illumined by the divine evaluation in Genesis 2:18, "It is not good that the man should be alone." Such a divine response to the creation up to this point assumes that evaluating the created order is an ongoing process, within which adjustments and even improvements can be made in view of the divine response and the engagement of the human. This is what happens in 2:19–22, with 2:23 constituting an evaluation by the *human*![9]

And what does it mean to be evaluated as *good*? The word "good" carries the sense of corresponding to the divine intention, including elements of beauty, purposefulness, and praiseworthiness. God observes a decisive continuity between God's intention and the creational result. At the same time, "good" does not mean static or perfect.[10] For most interpreters, the word "perfect" means something like "without fault, defect, or inadequacy, or in no need of improvement or development to be what it truly is." The word "good," however, is different in its basic sense and needs closer attention.

Several clues in the text demonstrate that "perfect" is not the appropriate way to assess the creational situation. For one, if the creation were perfect, how could anything go wrong, such as is reported in the chapters that follow? For another, the "not good" of Genesis 2:18 relative to the human being pushes in this direction of reflection; it suggests that creation is a process and that it moves *toward* "good." But the command to "subdue" the earth (1:28) is the clearest evidence for the claim.[11] This

9. See further discussion below. Moreover, such an evaluation by God has environmental implications. To use the language of Francis Watson, "Human acts which treat the nonhuman creation simply as the sphere of use-value or market-value, refusing the acknowledgment of its autonomous goodness, are *acts of terrorism* in direct opposition to the intention of the creator" (*Text, Church, World: Biblical Interpretation in Theological Perspective* [Grand Rapids: Eerdmans, 1994], 146–47, emphasis added).

10. For a discussion of the importance of God's being presented as an evaluator in Gen. 1, see Fretheim, *God and World*, 40–42.

11. One might also cite Gen. 3:16, which speaks of the "increase" of pain in childbirth, implying that pain would have been experienced in a pre-sin birth. Suffering is thus shown to be not necessarily related to sin, a point also made by

verb, used elsewhere in the Old Testament for coercive human activities against other humans (see 2 Sam. 8:11; Esther 7:8; Jer. 34:11), is never applied to relationships with creatures that are not human.[12] Moreover, the verb is here used in a pre-sin context, before any negative effects that sin has brought, and apparently no enemies are in view.[13] Given its use in a pre-sin context, one should be careful not simply to transfer the usage of the verb for post-sin human activity to an understanding of this word here. More seems to be at stake.

I have suggested that the best sense for the verb is "to bring order out of continuing disorder."[14] The command may have in view God's own pattern of acting relative to the already-existent "earth," as in Genesis 1:9–10: "Let the waters . . . be gathered together, . . . and let the dry land *appear*," which God called Earth. The command to "subdue" assumes that the earth was not fully developed, that there was not a once-for-all givenness to the creation at the end of the seventh day. The command is given in the service of developing God's creation toward its fullest possible potential. God's creation is a dynamic reality and is going somewhere; it is a long-term project, ever in the process of becoming—as the history of nature shows, with the earth-changing activities of such creatures as glaciers, earthquakes, volcanoes, and tsunamis. This potential of becoming is built into the very structures of the world. For human beings to subdue the earth, together with the involvement of other creatures (see below), means that over time the creation would look quite different than it did on the seventh day. Somewhat ironically, God gives to the human being this "natural law" in order that the created order would *not* remain the same.

---

the book of Job (see below, chap. 3; see also Jesus' argument in John 9:1–3, which eliminates two possible sources for the blind man's suffering: his own sin and his parents' sin). See chap. 4, note 6, below.

12. The "land" is "subdued" in several texts (Num. 32:22, 29; Josh. 18:1; 1 Chron. 22:18), but that has reference to people who occupy the land.

13. Some scholars do understand that Gen. 1 reflects creation by means of conflict. For discussion, see Fretheim, *God and World*, 43–48.

14. See ibid., 52–53.

In other terms, Genesis does not present the creation as a finished product, wrapped up with a big red bow and handed over to the creatures to keep it exactly as originally created. It is not a onetime production. Indeed, for the creation to stay just as God originally created it would constitute a failure of the divine design. From God's perspective, the world needs work; development and change are what God intends for it, and God enlists human beings (and other creatures) to that end. From another angle, God did not exhaust the divine creativity in the first week of the world; God continues to create and uses creatures in a vocation that involves the becoming of creation.

The evaluation "good" is not taken away when sin enters the life of the world. Sin negatively affects the life of human beings, certainly, and through them the life of other creatures. But nowhere does Scripture take away the evaluation "good" from any creature. In the wake of sin many texts actually will reinforce that evaluation, sometimes in even stronger terms. With respect to human beings, God announces, "You are precious in my sight, and honored" (Isa. 43:5); God continues to regard them as "crowned . . . with glory and honor" (Ps. 8:5).

Though human beings certainly need to hear that they often think of themselves more highly than they ought to think, it is also important for them to hear that they often think of themselves *less* highly than they ought to think. To speak less highly of the human is to diminish the quality of God's own work. And this is the case not least because of such continuing *divine* evaluations of them as good. The creational commands in Genesis 1:28 and God's engagement with the human in 2:19–20 indicate that God values human beings, places confidence in them, and honors what they do and say, though not uncritically. Human words and deeds count; they make a difference to the world and to God, not least because God has chosen to use human agents in getting God's work done in the world (see below). We need constantly to be reminded that the godness of God cannot be bought at the expense of creaturely diminishment.

15

Another word that can be used to designate the goodness of creatures is "free."[15] One way in which the creation accounts witness to this reality is the seventh day of creation (Gen. 2:1–3); this day on which *God* rests (not human beings)[16] is testimony to God's suspension of creative activity, which allows the creatures, each in its own way, to be what they were created to be. God thereby gives to all creatures a certain independence and freedom. With regard to human beings, God leaves room for genuine decisions as they exercise their God-given power (see already 2:19). With regard to nonhuman creatures, God releases them from "tight divine control" and permits them to be themselves as the creatures they are.[17] The latter includes the becoming of creation, from the movement of tectonic plates to volcanic activity, to the spread of viruses, to the procreation of animals. This divine commitment to the creatures entails an ongoing divine constraint and restraint in the exercise of power, a divine commitment that we often wish had not been made, especially when suffering and death are in view.[18] But God will remain true to God's commitments, come what may.

From another angle, the divine *commands* of Genesis 1:28 (be fruitful, multiply, fill the earth, subdue, have dominion) are given for the sake of the future of the world. Law is thus understood as a pre-sin reality that is built into its creational structures. Concern for the future of the creation is made a matter of divine law from the very beginning. When Israel is later given the law, the people of God thereby are to understand that they stand in the tradition of *creational* law, and

15. One might distinguish between the freedom of humans and nonhumans with the terms "free will" and "free process." So John Polkinghorne, *Quarks, Chaos, and Christianity: Questions to Science and Religion* (New York: Crossroad, 1994), 46–47.

16. Later texts will call on human beings to rest as God rested, but not in Genesis (Exod. 20:8–11; 31:17).

17. So Polkinghorne, *Quarks*, 47. Sin surely complicates the understanding of freedom, as does the influence of other creatures on our ways of being and doing.

18. For further reflection on this theme, see below.

16

that they are caught up by God in a vocation that involves, among other things, the becoming of creation.[19]

And so God creates a dynamic world in which the future is open to a number of possibilities and in which creaturely activity is crucial for proper creational developments. In other words, God chooses to establish an interdependent relationship with the creation; God chooses to work with others in creating. Certain constants are in place: seedtime and harvest, cold and heat, summer and winter, day and night (Gen. 8:22). But beyond that, the future of the world is characterized by a remarkable open-endedness, in which more than God is involved (see below).

Thinking about the Creator God

How we think about the Creator God of Genesis 1–2 will sharply affect how we carry on this conversation.[20] It is almost a chorus among commentators that God created the world alone, with overwhelming power and absolute control, while working independently and unilaterally. Making such claims about the Creator God constitutes a practical end of the conversation for many interpreters.

But if this understanding of the imaging of God in Genesis 1 is correct, then those created in God's image (so Gen. 1:26) could *properly* understand their role regarding the rest of creation in comparable terms: in terms of power over, absolute control, and independence. By definition, the natural world thus becomes available for human manipulation and exploitation. Thus, if all the creatures of Genesis 1 are understood to be but passive putty in the hands of God, does that not invite a comparable treatment of them by those created in the image of such a God? In other words, how we image the

19. For an extended consideration of creation and law, see Fretheim, *God and World*, 133–56.
20. These next paragraphs build on ibid., 48–49.

God of the creation accounts will have a significant impact on our view of the world, our environmental sensitivities, and the urgency of our practices.

What if the God of the creation accounts is imaged more as one who, in creating, chooses to share power? Then the way in which the human as image of God exercises dominion is to be shaped by that model. Even more, if the God of the creation accounts is imaged as one who also involves *nonhuman* creatures in still further creations, as we will see, then that should inform our understanding of the value, indeed great value, that they have been given by God.

Although creatures are deeply dependent on God for their creation and life, God has chosen to establish an *interdependent* relationship with creatures with respect to both originating creation and continuing creation.[21] God's approach to creation is communal, relational, and in the wake of God's initiating activity, God works from within the world rather than on the world from without (cf. chap. 5, below). God's word in creation is often a communicating with others, rather than a top-down word.[22] The creation texts thus show a sharp interest on God's part in sharing creative activity.

This idea may be conveyed as well by the presentation of the creation of the world in terms of actual days, with evening and morning explicitly and repeatedly developed. However literally one interprets the seven days, they are emblematic of any period of time that it takes for the creation to come

21. In Michael Welker's language, "In no way do the creation accounts of Genesis offer only a gloomy picture of sheer dependence. God's creative action does not confront that which is created with completely finished facts. The creature's own activity is a constitutive element in the process of creation and that is seen to be in harmony with God's action" ("What Is Creation: Rereading Genesis 1 and 2," *Theology Today* 48 [1991]: 64).

22. Though the biblical testimony, finally, witnesses to creation out of nothing (2 Maccabees 7:28; Rom. 4:17; Heb. 11:3), there is strong consensus that this idea is only on the edges of Gen. 1–2 in several details (e.g., the creation of light, firmament, and luminaries) and not a reference to creation as a whole.

into being and develop.[23] Such language suggests that the creation of the universe takes time, even for God. Efforts to claim that God created the universe instantaneously have long been made (e.g., Augustine). Certainly the all-powerful God would not need to take any time to bring the world into being! In some fundamental sense, however, the text presents God as bringing the world into being over time. The result is that creation is seen as a dynamic process and not simply a product. This text suggests that God, who involves the creatures themselves in further creational developments (as we will see), takes the time necessary for the creation to come to be.

The Modes of Creation

In another context I have sought to lay out the various modes of creation that God uses in the Old Testament.[24] I am concerned here to highlight (and somewhat reshape) four of those modes of thinking in such a way as to emphasize the *communal* angle of vision regarding creation: (1) God uses already-existing creatures as material for creating new creatures; (2) God invites nonhuman creatures to participate in creation; (3) God invites the divine assembly to be coparticipant in the creation of the human; (4) God gives to the human being an important role in further creating activity.

God as Creator works in and through the creative capacities of that which is not God. What human and nonhuman creatures do in creation counts with respect to the emergence of ever-new creations; they make a difference regarding the shape that the future of the creation takes. Indeed, it could be said that their activity makes a difference to God's future with creation.

---

23. Note that Exod. 20:11; 31:17 seem to understand that the six days are literal. See Fretheim, *God and World*, 61–64.
24. Compare the list of eleven modes in ibid., 34–35.

19

1. God's Use of Already-Existing Matter in Creating

I begin by noting Genesis 1:2 and the role of the spirit/ wind/breath of God (the ambiguity should be retained) with respect to the "formless void," yet consisting of creatures such as earth and water. The spirit of God "moves, sweeps over" the face of the waters; this image suggests creative action that has an ever-changing velocity and direction.[25] The spirit works with already-existing matter; in fact, much of what is created in the balance of Genesis 1 is created out of material already present in Genesis 1:2.[26] Out of the mess of Genesis 1:2 (understood as chaos/disorder, not evil)[27] comes the orderliness of 1:3–31—though not without some continuing disorder (see, e.g., the omission of certain words and phrases in its normally regular structure).[28] The spirit works in the disorder of things to bring about new life and new order, an order that is not precise or tightly woven, despite initial appearances.[29] The spirit of God and raw material of a most earthy sort are brought together, and creation is animated (see Ps. 104:30).

25. This language is used for a drunken walk in Jer. 23:9. See John 3:8, "The wind blows where it chooses."
26. See Wisdom of Solomon 11:17, God "created the world out of formless *matter*" (emphasis added).
27. For detail, see Fretheim, *God and World*, 43–46.
28. For example, J. Richard Middleton, *The Liberating Image: The Imago Dei in Genesis 1* (Grand Rapids: Brazos, 2005), has shown that considerable variation exists within the seven-day structure of Gen. 1 (the variety includes eight creative acts in six days; the "let us" relates only to the creation of the human). Middleton says, "Whereas the world rhetorically depicted in Genesis 1 is certainly ordered, patterned, and purposive, the God who is artisan and maker does not over-determine the order of the cosmos" (306n25). In other words, the work of the spirit issues in a creation that, for all of its orderliness, is characterized by openness and freedom and by continuing disorder.
29. "The God of the Bible is a storm, blowing us like leaves from what we are to what we will be and only knowing us in this motion. . . . God is transforming and faithful liveliness; God is Spirit" (Robert Jenson, *Christian Dogmatics*, ed. C. E. Braaten and R. W. Jenson [Philadelphia: Fortress, 1984], 1:173–74). God gives to creation the continuing capacity not only to be itself, to be what it was created to be, but also to develop into something more. The Spirit enables becoming, enables genuine novelty to emerge.

This language suggests liveliness, movement, energy, change, and open-endedness. A remarkable imaging of God in the opening verses of the Bible! This spirit image of creation signals a dynamic rather than a static creative process, an open process rather than one that is tightly controlled.

Eugene Peterson speaks of "the mess of creativity": "I can never be involved in creativity except by entering the mess. Mess is the precondition of creativity."[30] He adds that risks abound in every creative enterprise; indeed, risk is essential to the meaning of creativity. False starts, failures, frustrations, embarrassments—all seem to be integral to the creative process. But out of the mess, love and beauty and peace often slowly emerge. Creative activity is itself finally unmanageable. When the spirit of God is at work, you cannot apply time management techniques or hire efficiency experts. To be a creator entails an almost infinite tolerance of messiness, of inefficiency. The moment that tidiness and strict orderliness become the rule of the day, creativity is inhibited and the appearance of the genuinely new slows way down.[31] Natural disasters come into view!

These reflections suggest that for the proper development of creation, some disorder must persist in the wake of God's originating creative activity. Sibley Towner puts it well: "If there were no freedom in the creation, no touches of disorder, no open ends, then moral choice, creativity, and excellence

30. Eugene Peterson, *Under the Unpredictable Plant: An Exploration in Vocational Holiness* (Grand Rapids: Eerdmans, 1994), 63.

31. See these scattered phrases in Penelope Green's article "Saying Yes to Mess" (*New York Times*, December 21, 2006):

[Irwin Kula said:] "It's a flippant remark, but if you've never had a messy kitchen, you've probably never had a home-cooked meal." . . . Mess is robust and adaptable . . . as opposed to brittle. . . . Mess is complete, in that it embraces all sorts of random elements. Mess tells a story: you can learn a lot about people from their detritus, whereas neat—well, neat is a closed book. Neat has no narrative. . . . Mess is also natural . . . and a real time-saver. [Mr. Freedman and Mr. Abrahamson write:] "It takes extra effort to neaten up a system. . . . Things generally don't neaten themselves." . . . [See] Einstein's oft-quoted remark, "If a cluttered desk is a sign of a cluttered mind, of what, then, is an empty desk?" (http://www.nytimes.com/2006/12/21/garden/21mess.html)

21

could not arise. The world would be a monotonous cycle of inevitability, a dull-as-dishwater world of puppets and automatons."[32] The mess of creativity is necessary rather than a meticulous blueprint. God, as it were, does not paint by numbers. God gives to creation the continuing capacity not only to be itself, to be what it was created to be, but also to develop into something more. The spirit, working in and through existing matter and other creatures, enables becoming, enables genuine novelty to emerge. While the Genesis text speaks of the spirit in terms of originating creation, Psalm 104:30 speaks of the spirit in terms of continuing creation: "When you send forth your spirit, they are created [*bara*]; and you renew the face of the ground" (see also Job 33:4; 34:14–15; 37:10). But in both cases, already-existing creatures are drawn into the creative process, and the effects are similar.

This theme of God's creating in and through existing messy matter continues in Genesis 2; in the creative process, God comes incredibly close to that which is earthy in molding the human being out of dirt. This verse paints a wonderful image of God. God gets down on the ground, takes on the stuff of creation, and gathers and shapes the dust into a human being—getting dirt under the divine fingernails, as it were. The ground (*'adamah*, a play on *'adam*) proves to be a crucial ingredient for the creation of the human. Human beings are not created "out of nothing," but out of an already-existent nonhuman creature, a creature that has creative capacities (see Gen. 1:11–13, 20, 24). God is imaged as a potter who molds a human being (and animals, Gen. 2:19) out of the dust of the earth (Gen. 2:7–8; see also Job 33:6; Pss. 103:14; 139:15; Isa. 45:9; 64:8; Jer. 18:1–6) and breathes into this new creature the breath of life. Moreover, God is imaged as a surgeon; God puts Adam to sleep, removes a part of his body (probably his side, not just a rib), and creates a woman (Gen. 2:22–23). A bloody process indeed! Such messiness

32. W. Sibley Towner, *Genesis* (Louisville: Westminster John Knox, 2001), 21.

is the way it commonly is in the process of creation. Once again, natural disasters come into view.

The testimony of Genesis 1 to the *goodness* of all forms of material reality is thus undergirded in Genesis 2 by God's *tangible and tactile* engagement with the creatures.[33] This text is testimony that finite, material realities are capable of being "handled" by God (see Ps. 95:5, "his hands . . . formed . . . the dry land"; Ps. 8:3, the heavens are "the work of your fingers") without compromising God's godness. Even more, if God is understood here to have taken on human form, implied by the nature of the actions (this divine move is explicit in Gen. 3:8), the stuff of creation actually bears God bodily in the life of the world. It is striking indeed that God, in creating the human being, assumes human form in so doing. The imaging of God in the form of a human being links this text with later theophanic passages (e.g., Gen. 18:1–2; Exod. 24:9–11).[34]

Moreover, God breathes God's own "breath of life" into the nostrils of a human being (Gen. 2:7) so that something of the very life of God comes to reside in the human. God the spirit fills the finite, human body with *divine* life (spirit and flesh need each other!). Even more, inasmuch as God repeats this breath-filled way of creating with respect to the animals (see 2:19; 7:15, 22), human beings do not have a monopoly on this divine way of creating. And so God here creates in a bodily and breathy way, using already-existing material realities to bring new creatures into being and to give them vitality. God is present and active, but at the same time

33. See Francis Watson, *Text, Church, World: Biblical Interpretation in Theological Perspective* (Grand Rapids: Eerdmans, 1994), 144: "God indwells her creation, not in the form of a static, passive presence but an active, dynamic self-transcending movement towards the emergence and reproduction of life and breath."

34. For an extended study of the theological import of the theophanic texts, see Terence E. Fretheim, *The Suffering of God: An Old Testament Perspective* (Philadelphia: Fortress, 1984), 79–106. For Christians, the link between divine word (Gen. 1) and divine flesh (Gen. 2–4) is sharply evident in New Testament claims regarding the incarnation (John 1:14).

23

there is an open-endedness to the ongoing creative process, to which the work of the spirit testifies.

And so the world has developed ever since. This theme stands against any notion that continuing creation beyond Genesis 1–2 is really only "preservation" of that which was created out of nothing. Creation "out of something" is integral to the understanding of creation in Genesis 1–2, and this understanding of creation is a reality in the continuing development of the world. God continues to involve nondivine creatures in the creation of the world as God did "in the beginning."[35]

The common notion that the Creator is completely external to the creation in the creative process is not present here. Again, God is creating from within the world, not from without. God is bringing new creatures into being with the help of already-existing creatures. It is not that God *needs* help, but that God chooses to use agents in the creating process; creation continues to be developed by God in a relational and communal way. Conceivably, God could have simply spoken a word and poof! a new creature would have been brought into existence. But that is not God's way in this text. God chooses instead to involve already-existing creatures in creating further creatures. Once again, natural disasters come into view.

The environmental implications of God's creating in this earthy way are considerable. Among other things, these actions show that God deeply values the stuff of earthy life and understands that such creatures are indispensable for creation to develop into a more-complex reality, including human life. And inasmuch as this earthy stuff is of value to God, certainly it should be of value to human beings and all creatures. Even more, in view of the genealogical reference in Genesis 2:4 ("These are the generations of the heavens and the earth"), it could be claimed that the earth is understood to be an integral aspect of the human ancestral heritage,

35. For a more extended discussion of this issue, see Fretheim, *God and World*, 3–9.

24

with all the implications that the earth has for continuing human life.

2. God Calls on Already-Existing Creatures to Bring about New Creations

Already in Genesis 1, God calls on the nonhuman creatures to bring about further acts of creating. On days 3, 5, and 6, God invites the creatures to be involved in further creative acts. For example, in Genesis 1:11–13, God invites, "Let the earth bring forth" (KJV), and we are told, "The earth brought forth." The earth is the subject of the creating verbs. And then on days 5 and 6, God invites the waters and the earth to bring forth further creatures. In these cases, God is the subject of the creating verb that follows, but given the pattern established by 1:11–13, this formulation does not take away from the coparticipation of the waters and the earth in those acts of creation.[36]

What happens in these cases is best characterized as mediate rather than immediate creative activity. Here God's creating is not presented as a unilateral act; it is multilateral. God's creating is not done alone; God recruits assistance from the creatures in creating. God chooses interdependence rather than independence. In this case, the nonhuman creatures have a genuine vocational role in enabling the creation to develop into something ever new. That story has certainly been repeated again and again over the millennia as ever-new creatures come into being, mediated by the activity of exist-

36. Grammatically, the use of the jussive "let" means that God's speaking does not function as command. It leaves room for creaturely response, not unlike the way the cohortative "Let us make" (Gen. 1:26) leaves room for consultation and the "Let them have dominion" (1:28, my trans.) entails a sharing of power (see below). The "let" associated with the luminaries (1:14–15) entails giving over to them the governance of the temporal realities of days, seasons, and years. God's governance is not unilateral, but mediated. Hence, the divine speaking in this chapter is of such a nature that the receptor of the word is important in the shaping of the created order.

25

ing creatures, from glaciers to volcanoes to earthquakes to tsunamis. Much of the beauty that we see in the natural world around us is due to the activity of such nonhuman creatures. Indeed, some of the most spectacular vistas of the natural order are due to the activity of such nonhuman creatures (e.g., mountains and valleys carved out by glacial movement). Natural disasters once again appear on the scene.

Moreover, it is not only human beings who are blessed and invited to be fruitful, to multiply, and to fill the earth; earlier, on day 5 (Gen. 1:22) animals are also called to do that. God here shares creative powers with that which is not human, enabling a significant point of commonality between human and nonhuman. Such creative capacities are thus determined by God not to be a uniquely human prerogative; God gives power over to the nonhuman to propagate their own kind. God thereby chooses to exercise an ongoing restraint and constraint in relationship to their future. So God will not suspend the created orders and relieve creatures of these procreational "responsibilities." God will not intervene in their "life" to make sure they are doing their job; God will allow these creatures to be what they were created to be—regardless. Thus God has not brought into being a ready-made world, but God has made a world in which creatures could make themselves. But it can become messy, as natural disasters show.

In portraying the creation of the world in such terms— letting the world create itself—these texts are a witness to divine self-limitation. God limits the divine power and opens up space for chance and freedom. In terms of the text, God keeps the Sabbath day (Gen. 2:1–3).[37] The Sabbath is a break from creating for God or, more precisely, a divine move to a different sort of creating (God "finished" on that day, 2:2). Resting on God's part means giving time and space over to the creatures to be what they were created to be: God will

[handwritten margin notes: "interesting thought", "Needs More thought", "But Cool"]

37. See the discussion of the Sabbath text in view of other studies, in Fretheim, *God and World,* 61–64.

26

be present and active in the world but will not be invested in the management of the creatures. God will rest and let them be and become what they were created to be, without divine interference, with all the capacities that they have been given. God rests so that the creatures can freely thrive (note that creatures do *not* rest in this text; that is only a later connection). God does not create with strings attached or keep creatures on a leash.[38] In such a divine allowance, God limits both the divine power and the divine freedom because God is committed to the structures of creation and their freedom.[39]

As we have recognized above, for the earth and the waters to so participate in creation inevitably means that the process is going to be disorderly and messy. This reality opens up the issue of suffering.[40] Much suffering will follow in the wake of the world's becoming. Earth and waters are not machines that work in precise and predictable and orderly ways. God has created a dynamic world; earthquakes, volcanoes, storms, bacteria, and viruses have their role to play in the becoming of the world—in both a pre-sin world and a post-sin world. These creatures function in an orderly process in many ways, but randomness also plays a role; in the words of Ecclesiastes 9:11, "Time and chance happen to them all." Because humans are part of this interconnected world, we may get in the way of the workings of these creatures and be hurt by them. This potential for "natural evil" was present from the beginning of the creation.[41]

What are the environmental implications of God calling on existing nonhuman creatures to bring about still other creatures, indeed entirely new creatures? Once again, the text

38. See Jürgen Moltmann, *God in Creation: A New Theology of Creation and the Spirit of God* (Minneapolis: Fortress, 1991), 88: "God does not create merely by calling something into existence, or by setting something afoot. In a more profound sense he 'creates' by letting-be, by making room, and by withdrawing himself."
39. From another angle, Gen. 2:1–3 is witness to the temporality of God. See Fretheim, *God and World*, 63.
40. See chap. 4, on suffering.
41. See chap. 3, on Job.

demonstrates the immense value of nonhuman creatures *for God* in that God involves them in the creation of still further creatures. Without the help of these nonhuman beings, God's creation would not live up to its potential of becoming.

3. God Invites the Divine Council to Participate in the Creation of the Human

We move to Genesis 1:26, "Let us make humankind in our image."[42] The range of God's involvement in creative activity with those who are not God is hereby extended. A remarkable majority of scholars understand this plural in terms of the divine council, the heavenly assembly that engages the deity and does God's bidding.[43] In addressing the divine assembly, God chooses not to create humankind alone, but with the aid of those beings who are not God. This divine council offers interrelated understandings regarding (1) the identity of God and (2) the creative activity of God.

a. *The identity of God.* Israel understands that God is by nature a social being, functioning within a divine community that is rich and complex. God is not in heaven alone and, even more, is engaged in a relationship of mutuality within that realm. In other words, relationship is integral to the identity of God, prior to and independent of God's relationship to the world. So when God decides to work communally in creation, God is being faithful to God's own self.

This divine council is also the most natural addressee of the words by God in Genesis 2:18: "It is not good that the man should be alone." This likely context recognizes that aloneness is not characteristic of God, and hence the isolated human being would not truly be created in the divine image. Or in different terms, it is not good for the human being to be

---

42. For more detail and other studies, see Fretheim, *God and World*, 42–43.
43. See, e.g., Patrick Miller, *Genesis 1–11: Studies in Structure and Theme* (Sheffield: JSOT Press, 1978). See also Isa. 6:8; Jer. 23:18–22.

alone because it would not be good for God either. Only the human being as social and relational to other human beings is truly correspondent to the sociality of God and what it means to be created in the image of God. The later witness that God is one (e.g., Deut. 6:4) is not compromised by this recognition of the sociality of God, for the divine beings in the assembly are not other gods.[44]

When the human is isolated and alone, in God's own words, it is "not good." Human beings are not autonomous creatures; they are defined by their relations to others. Moreover, given the democratization inherent in the use of the image of God language (Gen. 1:26–27)—including all human beings, regardless of gender, race, or class—means that human beings are not to rule over one another.[45]

God's choosing not to create alone is revealing of a divine vulnerability. For in so involving those who are not God, room is given for the messy activity of finite creatures. In making such moves, God takes risks.

b. *The creative activity of God.* In addressing the divine assembly with "Let us make," God specifically chooses to share the creative process with those who are not God. God determines not to create humankind alone, but to share the responsibility for creating with the already-created. Once again, God chooses to use agents other than God's own self. Such a communal, creative move is especially important in this case because it is crucial for the very nature of the human. In other terms, given

44. These plural references to God have been interpreted by Christians as trinitarian. But it is historically more accurate to say that these Old Testament perspectives regarding the social nature of God provided a theological matrix for the development of later theological perspectives. See Terence E. Fretheim, "Christology and the Old Testament," in *Who Do You Say That I Am? Essays on Christology*, ed. Mark A. Powell and David Bauer (Louisville: Westminster John Knox, 1999), 201–15. Early Christian reflections about God that led to trinitarian thought were not merely grounded in New Testament claims about Jesus and the Holy Spirit.

45. The "rule" of Gen. 3:16 is due to the entrance of sin into the life of the world and entails a distortion of God's original intention. See Phyllis Trible, *God and the Rhetoric of Sexuality* (Philadelphia: Fortress, 1978).

29

the divine decision to create humankind in the image and likeness of God, all that it means to be divine must be at work in the creating of that image. This reality may be reflected in the use of the phrases "our image" and "our likeness" (Gen. 1:26).

We especially notice the introduction of readers to a divine community at precisely the point of the creation of the human community. The creation of the human community is thereby shown to be the result of a dialogical act or an inner-divine consultation rather than a monological move—a frequent way that scholars have presented the God of creation in Genesis 1. God certainly takes the initiative and extends the invitation to the divine council, but their participation is not understood to be of little or no consequence. These heavenly creatures have a genuine role to play in creation. Interaction and mutual interdependence are once again characteristic of God's creative activity. What might it mean for the care of the environment that human beings are fundamentally relational and creative beings?

Hence, if we do not use genuine relational language in our talk about God's creative activity, then that may adversely affect how we think about the human as being created in the image of God. For example, it could mean understanding human relationality only in a perfunctory sense and reckoning human involvement in matters of creation to be of no special import.

4. God Involves the Human in Still Further Acts of Creation.

In Genesis 1, God is imaged most basically as a Creator and, as we have seen in the above sections, God is one who acts relationally in that capacity. This being the case, creativity and relationality become fundamental descriptors of those created in the image of God, which in turn help to shape the tasks to which they have been called relative to the earth. In other terms, inasmuch as human beings are created in the

30

image of a Creator God, they themselves must be understood as creators as well.

a. *Genesis 2:4–5, 15.* "In the day that the LORD God made the earth and the heavens, . . . no plant . . . was yet in the earth, . . . and there was no one to till [better, "serve"] the ground." Human activity is deemed to be essential if the creation is to become what God intended it to be. Here human beings are given a crucial role in the initial stages of the creation of the world. God decides not to retain all power relative to the new creation (see on Sabbath above). The responsibility in 2:5 "to till the ground" has creation-wide reference; in 2:15 that responsibility will have more-particular reference to the "garden of Eden."

b. *Genesis 1:28 (4:1; 5:1–3).* Be fruitful, multiply, fill the earth, have dominion, subdue the earth.[46] God's initial word to the human being in 1:28 is striking, coming as it does from the mouth of God. This divine move constitutes a sharing of power. God gives the human being certain tasks and responsibilities and, necessarily, the power with which to do them. From the beginning, God chooses not to be the only one who has creative power and the capacity, indeed the obligation, to exercise it. Given the imaging of God as one who creates, these words of commission should be interpreted fundamentally in terms of *creative and communal word and deed.* Human beings are invited to play an important role in the becoming of their world, indeed, bringing into being that which is genuinely new.[47] As we have noticed, it is important to observe that these charges in Genesis 1:28 are made a matter of (pre-sin) law. Such a way of stating human responsibilities stresses the importance of these matters *for God.*

46. For an earlier discussion of these verbs and texts, see Fretheim, *God and World,* 49–61.

47. See Jürgen Moltmann, *The Future of Creation: Collected Essays* (Philadelphia: Fortress, 1979), 120: "Creation at the beginning is the creation of conditions for the potentialities of creation's history, . . . of constructive and destructive possibilities. . . . We cannot see in initial creation the invariant nature of history, but we can see the beginning of nature's history."

God certainly takes the initiative in distributing this power to the creatures, and God is the one who invites their participation in the use of power. But having done so, God is committed to this way of relating to them, and forfeiting or suspending this status for shorter or longer periods of time is not a divine option. God is a power-sharing God, indeed a creation-sharing God, and God will be faithful to that way of relating to those created in the divine image. Let us take a closer look at several of the verbs of Genesis 1:28:

Be fruitful, multiply, fill the earth. If creative power is an essential element in the imaging of God, then human likeness to God in one respect consists in our procreative capacity (also true of animals; see Gen. 1:22).[48] Indeed, procreation is stated as a human obligation for the sake of continuity in creation. To that end, God builds into the very structure of these creatures the capacity to generate new life.[49] By being what they were created to be and without the need for divine intervention, they can "naturally" be productive of new life and perpetuate their own kind. God is present in the process (see Ps. 139:13), but not in a managerial way that would keep human decisions and actions from counting or potentially random events from wreaking havoc (the randomness of the gene pool). Humans will do the procreating, not God! Reproduction is a responsibility that human beings have in order to be the image of God they were created to be.[50]

Genesis 4:1. When the first human child is born, Eve gives a *theological* interpretation of what has occurred: She has

---

48. Human beings are the only creatures capable of being evaluators as God has been throughout Gen. 1, continuing to invest value in the world as God has done.

49. Phyllis Bird thinks of this divine move in polemical terms, as undercutting the importance of the fertility-cult activities; no activity of the gods is needed for perpetuating the agricultural year or the species (*Missing Persons and Mistaken Identities: Women and Gender in Ancient Israel* [Minneapolis: Fortress, 1997], 137–38).

50. Compare the "responsibility" given to the luminaries as part of their creation (Gen. 1:14–16); they are to "rule" and to distinguish days and seasons, for the sake of "the earth" (1:15, 17).

"*created* a man with the help of the LORD" (my trans.).[51] Eve is the decisive agent here, the subject of the verb of creation; she is the *creator* of this new man-child, the first human subject of a creating verb. Up to this point, only God has been involved in the creation of human beings. Eve recognizes that in giving birth she has been caught up by God in a continu- ation of that creative work. Her unusual reference to having created a "man" (*'ish*) rather than a child expresses her creative continuity with Adam's interpretation of God's action in 2:23 that woman was taken out of "man" (*'ish*). Here the man is taken out of the woman. *// So Cool*

Genesis 5:1–3. This passage continues the theme. As God has created humankind in the divine image and likeness, so Adam creates ("became the father of") Seth in his "likeness" and "image."[52] Strikingly, God's creation of humankind in the image of God is placed as the first generation within an extensive genealogy. This link suggests that human procreation is understood to be a genuinely creative act and finds its true parallel in God's own creative activity. In the language of the text, human beings have now assumed the role of creating the image of God, or more precisely, still further images of God, each of whom would carry on God's own breath of life into successive generations (2:7; cf. 9:6). In other words, the story of human generation that now follows in Genesis 5 stands directly in the tradition of God's creative activity (see above on God's resting).

Subdue the earth; have dominion. To summarize our earlier consideration of this point: for the human being to "subdue" entails intra-creational development, bringing order out of continuing disorder, drawing the world along to its fullest possible creational potential.[53] Creation is thus understood to be, not

51. For the use of the verb *qanah* for *divine* creation, see Gen. 14:19–22.

52. See Dexter Callender, *Adam in Myth and History: Ancient Israelite Perspectives on the Primal Human* (Winona Lake, IN: Eisenbrauns, 2000), 32–33. Note that in Gen. 5:1–3 "image" and "likeness" are reversed from 1:26.

53. See also Fretheim, *God and World*, 48–53.

a static state of affairs that God has brought into being, but a highly dynamic situation in which human activity will prove to be crucial for the proper development of the created order (see below on Gen. 2:18–20). That God has entrusted human beings with such godlike responsibility is witness to their having been "crowned . . . with glory and honor" (Ps. 8:5).

Human beings are also created to "have dominion" (*radab*) over "every living thing that moves upon the earth" (Gen. 1:26, 28). The language of dominion apparently was drawn from the sphere of ideal conceptions of royal responsibility (see Ezek. 34:1–4, where "force" and "harshness" are needed to qualify the verb; so also Lev. 25:43, 46). The verb should thus be understood in terms of caregiving, even nurturing, not exploitation (killing animals is a post-sin reality; Gen. 9:2–3). At the same time, in order to maintain the democratizing theme inherent in the image, the focus should be placed on what the king *does*, not who the king is. Every human being, without distinction of gender, class, or societal status, is to relate to nonhuman creatures as God would. And so, it is what *God* (not the human king) does that is the model for what humans are called to do. If God is imaged more as one who, in creating, chooses to share power in relationship, then the way in which the human as image of God exercises dominion is to be shaped by that model. Since the images of God as Creator in this chapter are fundamentally creative and relational, it seems out of place to focus on the image of dominion or sovereignty or rule in a traditional way.

c. *Genesis 2:18–20.* God here returns to the consultative mode, not unlike God's move with the divine council.[54] God catches up the *'adam* in the creative process, giving him the task of determining whether the animals will be a satisfactory resolution with respect to the issue of aloneness. In that creative and evaluative process of naming the animals, the

---

54. For an earlier formulation, see ibid., 56–60.

human is given the power to determine whether the animals will enable the creational situation to advance from "not good" to good, and in view of that human decision, to determine the rightness of the woman in meeting the issue of human aloneness.

That God's first move to address the issue of human aloneness is the creation of animals has long raised questions for interpreters. Does God think that the animals will meet the identified problem in some way? Is this a trial-and-error move for God? Though this divine initiative proves not to be a final decision, God's move must at least mean that the animals are understood by God to constitute a community that could address the issue of human aloneness. In other words, God gives to the animals a very high value in the shaping of human community.

At this point, God's role is the placing of various creative possibilities before the human being, giving the creature the freedom to decide. God lets the *human being* determine whether the animals are adequate to move the evaluation of the creation from "not good" to "good." The human being, not God, deems what is "fit for him." God will take seriously into account the creative human response in shaping the future of creation. The human decision corresponds to the divine evaluative rhythm of Genesis 1 ("and God saw that it was good"). Once again, creation is portrayed as process, not simply event.

God learns from what the human being actually does with the task that has been divinely assigned.[55] God accepts the human decision and goes back to the drawing boards. Divine decisions interact with human decisions in the creation of the world. Creation is process as well as punctiliar act; creation is creaturely as well as divine.

55. See Bruce Birch, "Creation and the Moral Development of God in Genesis 1–11," in *"And God Saw That It Was Good": Essays on Creation and God in Honor of Terence E. Fretheim*, ed. Frederick J. Gaiser and Mark Throntveit, Word & World Supplement Series 5 (St. Paul: Word & World, Luther Seminary, 2006), 12–22.

The future is genuinely open here. It depends on what the human being does with what God presents. Will the human being decide that the animals resolve the issue of aloneness? How the *human beings* in their God-given freedom decide will determine whether there will be a next human generation. In some basic sense, God places the very future of the human race in human hands (it will not be the last such divine gesture!), which will in turn shape the future of the world. Phyllis Trible has put this point in a helpful way: God is now present, "not as the authoritarian controller of events, but as the generous delegator of power who even forfeits the right to reverse human decisions."[56] W*hatever* the human being called each animal, "that was its name" (Gen. 2:19). Whatever!

The human being's naming of each creature is meant to be parallel to the divine naming in Genesis 1:5–10, though God names no living creatures; that is left up to the human. This act is not a perfunctory utilitarian move; naming is a part of the creative process itself, discerning the very nature of intra-creaturely relationships. It is not that human beings have the capacity to stymie God's movement into the future in any *final* way. But God has established a relationship with human beings such that their decisions about developments in creation truly count.[57]

God recognizes the creational import of the human decision, for no additional divine word or act is forthcoming. God lets the man's exultation over the woman fill the scene; in lieu of a statement from God, the *human word* (the first uttered in Genesis) counts for the evaluation that the creation is now "good."

These various texts place the issue of human responsibility for the future of creation directly on the plates of the

56. Trible, *God and the Rhetoric of Sexuality*, 93.

57. Is this much different from the contemporary situation, where (e.g.) human environmental (in)sensitivity may have a comparable import for the future of the world? Indeed, such decisions could put an end to the human race as decisively as Adam's choice of the animals as "partner" would have (Gen. 2:20).

creatures, especially human beings. We cannot rest back and assume that God will take care of everything or that the future of the creation is solely in God's hands. Ultimately it is, yes, but in the meantime, human beings are called not to passivity but to genuine engagement, and the decisions that we make will have significant implications for the future of the earth and the nature of the future of God.[58]

These various ways of "unpacking" the work of the Creator God have significant implications for the way in which the Old Testament understands how the world has come to be. Words such as "relational" and "communal" shape our perception of the coming-to-be of the natural order. God's creating is not done alone; God chooses interdependence rather than independence. The nonhuman creatures have a genuine vocational role in enabling the creation to develop into something ever new. That story has certainly been repeated again and again over the millennia as ever-new creatures come into being, mediated by the activity of existing creatures, from glaciers to volcanoes to earthquakes to tsunamis. Much of the beauty that we see in the natural world around us is due to the activity of such nonhuman creatures. Words such as "neat" and "orderly" are only in part descriptive of the creational process; themes such as "open-ended" and "messy" again and again come into view. Natural disasters may be messy indeed, but at the same time, they appear to be an integral part of God's way of bringing an ever-new creation into being—as also in the story of Noah and the flood, where the effects were surely made worse by human violence.

---

58. See Jer. 22:1–5 and the "if, if not" formulation. A number of such texts could be cited.

2

The God
of the Flood Story
and Natural Disasters

"Noah and the Ark" is often considered a classic children's story, and it has found its way into the design of many a baby's nursery and many a child's toy.[1] It is usually portrayed as a remarkably peaceful scene, as two by two the animals parade into the ark, and there is nary a cloud in the sky. In these uses of the flood story, a common assumption seems to be that the child will accompany the animals onto the ark, cuddle down in their mangers, and safely ride out the storm. Rarely today are we shown images of those children

1. For an earlier version of these reflections, see Terence E. Fretheim, "The God of the Flood Story and Natural Disasters," *Calvin Theological Journal* 43 (2008): 21–34. For an analysis of the neglected place given to children in the Bible, see Danna Nolan Fewell, *The Children of Israel: Reading the Bible for the Sake of Our Children* (Nashville: Abingdon, 2003).

who did not happen to be members of Noah's family and are swept away in the deluge, never to be heard from again. What if Noah, like Abraham, had argued with God on behalf of the children?

Questions abound about the flood story, not least regarding theological issues. How shall we speak of the God of this story? How shall we speak of suffering and death that is caused by natural disasters in that world and in our own? Is this different from the suffering and death caused by moral evil (say, 9/11), and if so, how? And is God's relationship to these "evils" different? If so, how? Many would claim that such "unnatural" events are at least in part due to human activities that have disrupted the delicate balance of the earth's ecosystem. The truth of such a claim is commonly accepted, both within and without the church. But is such an "explanation" sufficient?

For those who believe in a living and active God, further questions must be asked: How might *God* be involved in these natural events and to what end? Even for those who are properly reserved in making theological claims about environmental events, these questions are important, not least because many biblical texts link divine judgment with natural catastrophe. In addition to the flood narrative (Gen. 6–8), one thinks of Sodom and Gomorrah (Gen. 18–19) or the plagues in Egypt (Exod. 7–12). Although each of these stories cites sinful human behavior for what happens to the ecosystem, God is certainly portrayed as deeply involved. Indeed, doesn't God make matters worse? For all the talk about God being committed to the stewardship of the earth, in these stories we find God contributing to the degradation of the environment![2]

Some interpreters of the current world scene are not hesitant in claiming a link between divine judgment and such

2. Many other texts could be cited, especially in the Prophets (e.g., Jer. 4:22–26).

disasters. They point to the depletion of the ozone layer and global warming, "unnatural" developments in the animal world, the spread of deadly diseases, and weather patterns that seem uncommonly violent, and they name them as the judgment of God. Aside from the heightened rhetoric and undisciplined certainty that often accompany such claims, is there a kernel of truth in the linkage of such phenomena to the judgmental activity of God? Even those who don't draw such conclusions and who recognize our inadequate knowledge of the history of nature and the difficulties of comparing disasters have often been given to a nagging bewilderment regarding such events. What *are* we to make of all the natural disasters that are a regular part of our world? Do we name them all in terms of God's judgment, in whole or in part, or just sometimes, and if so, how do we draw distinctions? All of this begs the question of what it means to speak of the judgment of God (see below).

From another angle, one is given to wonder about the nature of God's good creation. Can "good" include natural disasters, as we have suggested? Most would grant that God's good creation was from "the beginning" characterized by "wildness," randomness, risks (e.g., water; the law of gravity), and the potential for ever-new developments in the natural order (cf. Job 38–41). Indeed, such natural events as earthquakes, volcanoes, floods, destructive weather patterns, cell mutations, and even potentially deadly viruses were certainly an integral part of the creation before human beings showed up. So in some sense, such potentially destructive natural events are God-designed in the very creation of things. Then, when human beings did show up, they were told to "subdue the earth" (Gen. 1:28), which must mean that, for all its goodness, the world was not tranquil and perfect (see chap. 1). And what might it mean for God not to keep all power for the divine self, but to share such subduing power with the newly created human beings and to invite nonhuman creatures to be involved in creation?

41

When sin entered the picture and that power was misused, we are told almost immediately that it had negative effects on the natural order, as thorns and thistles complicated the farmer's vocation and the pain of childbirth was *increased* (Gen. 3:16–19). There was potential for pain and suffering in the pre-sin world.[3] As for the flood, it is directly related to human (and animal) violence in Genesis 6:11–13, which had the effect of corrupting the *earth* that God had created. And so, the flood is an ecological disaster directly related to the moral order, to human behaviors. In more general terms, such texts are testimony to the highly interrelated world in which we live, in which every creaturely move affects every other creature for good or for ill. But sin intensifies the negative dimensions of this interrelatedness. One might ask: Is the flood in itself the effect of human violence, or is it the range and intensity of the flood? Certainly the latter.

In today's world, a clear distinction would have to be made between moral-order events such as 9/11 and cosmic-order events such as the tsunamis—but not an absolute distinction. We need to ask: Given the interrelated spiderweb of a world in which we live (cf. chap. 5, below), has not human sin had an adverse effect on at least some natural events? Think of Katrina, for example, from the perspective of inadequate human preparations and responses, the classism evident in the disproportionate suffering of the lower rungs of that culture, and the possible effects of global warming on the storm's severity. If at least some such natural events can be so understood, where moral order and natural order are linked, it is difficult to deny an interpretation of such events at least partially in terms of God's judgment, not least if one understands judgment as the effects or consequences of sin. Again, issues of discernment are immediately at hand, and divine judgment needs closer definition (see below).

3. For a discussion of suffering as a part of God's good creation, see Douglas J. Hall, *God and Human Suffering: An Exercise in the Theology of the Cross* (Minneapolis: Augsburg, 1986), 53–67.

And so, in considering such disasters, we cannot let God off the hook. Assigning some responsibility to God for these events is important from at least two perspectives. On the one hand, such natural disasters are an integral part of God's creational design; on the other hand, human sin may make specific natural events more severe—in connection with which one might, and indeed (from a biblical perspective) *must*, speak of divine judgment. In either case, God cannot be removed from some kind of complicity. And so we will need to ask further about the God of the flood story and how that portrayal might inform our consideration of natural disasters in our own time.

Interpretations of the Flood Story

Before I do that theological work, I look more closely at the flood story and the various interpretive issues it has raised. Many books and articles have been written from across the spectrum of interpretive and theological commitments in an effort to sort out the issues.[4] I introduce only a few of them here.

1. *The present literary form*. We could track the relationship between the biblical flood story and other flood stories, particularly in the ancient Near East, such as the Atrahasis Epic or the Epic of Gilgamesh, flood stories that are most closely related to the biblical version. We could delineate the more proximate literary sources of the biblical story, including the Yahwistic and Priestly versions and their redactional history. But for these purposes I simply recognize that the present story is a composite text, with a complex literary history, and I will work with the final form of the text.

2. *The geology of the flood*. My interest in this article is not historical or archaeological, but I pass along a few comments

4. See the collection of essays edited by F. García Martínez and G. P. Lut-tikhuizen, *Interpretations of the Flood* (Leiden: Brill, 1998); David Pleins, *When the Great Abyss Opened: Classic and Contemporary Readings of Noah's Flood* (Oxford: Oxford University Press, 2003).

regarding a recent study.[5] Ryan and Pitman argue that the current shoreline of the Black Sea was created about 5600 BCE, when a flood from the Mediterranean Sea poured through the Bosporus to inundate an originally small, freshwater, inland sea. The flood refugees carried various stories of their experience throughout the region, one or more of which provided the literary inspiration for our flood story. This analysis certainly remains highly speculative, but it may contribute some insight into the text in a way that the common river-flooding hypothesis does not.[6] The discussion of flood geology is remarkably complex in its efforts to determine the relationship between various textual and scientific perspectives. I am only given to wonder why a certain interpretation of Scripture so often dictates how one reads the geological record.[7]

3. *Interpretations of the flood.* Also of interest are the various interpretations of the biblical flood story through the centuries. The New Testament most often views the flood story typologically. For example, the flood was viewed as

5. For a recent effort, see William Ryan and Walter Pitman, *Noah's Flood: The New Scientific Discoveries about the Event That Changed History* (New York: Simon & Schuster, 2000); and the review in Pleins, *When the Great Abyss Opened*, 3–14.

6. The many efforts to find Noah's ark have proved it to be elusive, with many unsubstantiated tales circulating through the centuries, and all discovered wood has been shown by carbon 14 dating to be from CE, not BCE. See Lloyd Bailey, *Noah: The Person in History and Tradition* (Columbia: University of South Carolina Press, 1989).

7. It is also possible to be so concerned that the Bible conform to the latest in scientific information that the interpretation of the text is skewed. Pleins (*When the Great Abyss Opened*) considers the major ways of relating the scientific and religious perspectives that scholars have taken over the centuries. The "exact literalist" takes the flood story at face value, no matter what scientific discoveries may show up; the "loose literalist" seeks to harmonize the biblical story and scientific analysis (e.g., the flood covered the world that was known then, not the entire world). Still others focus on a mythic interpretation: one takes a secularist approach; the other seeks enduring truths about the world. Questions about the historicity of the flood and the wholesale destruction of human beings and animals are not new to the modern world (see Louis Feldman, "Questions about the Great Flood, as Viewed by Plato, Pseudo-Philo, Josephus, and the Rabbis," *Zeitschrift für die alttestamentliche Wissenschaft* 115 [2003]: 401–22).

a prefiguring of the end times (e.g., Matt. 24:37–39; 2 Pet. 3:5–10). As Noah was saved from the deluge by means of the ark, so also will believing Christians be saved by God when the end unexpectedly comes. In early Christian interpretations, the ark came to symbolize the church, built on such texts as 1 Peter 3:20–21, where the saving of Noah and his household through water prefigured baptism, being saved through water. From another angle, Noah was viewed as the exemplar of one who was faithful to God; in the words of 2 Peter 2:5, Noah was a "herald of righteousness" (see Heb. 11:7 on the faith of Noah). Noah even became a type of Christ in some interpretations, prefiguring the resurrection.[8]

Various more whimsical, if altogether serious, interpretations of the story have appeared over the centuries.[9] For example, the shape of the ark and the arrangement of the living spaces on the ark were concerns. One depiction surmised that there were some 900 compartments on the ark, each 6 cubits square, arranged in 6 rows, with 3 corridors of 4 cubits' width. Also of interest has been the kind of animals on the ark and what to do about the carnivores and the insects. The nature of the food that was eaten by the ark's occupants has been explored, from dried figs to foods suitable for each species aboard; indeed, one estimate included 146,000 cubic cubits of hay. Various efforts were made to resolve the difficulties faced by Noah and his family in feeding all the animals and how the animal waste was gathered and disposed of (one

8. The effect on the liturgies of the church has been considerable. An oft-used baptismal prayer reads in part: "Almighty and everlasting God, who of thy great mercy didst save Noah and his family in the ark from perishing by water, . . . so also may this child be received into the ark of Christ's church, and being steadfast in faith, joyful through hope, and rooted in charity, may so pass through the waves of this troublesome world, that finally he may come to the land of everlasting life." For one such version, see Bard Thompson, *Book of Prayers for Church and Home* (Philadelphia: Christian Education, 1962), 77.

9. For many such details, see Pleins, *When the Great Abyss Opened*; Norman Cohn, *Noah's Flood: The Genesis Story in Western Thought* (New Haven: Yale University Press, 1996).

estimate was placed at 12 tons a day!). One could go on and on: to a striking extent the often-unbridled human imagination has been engaged in filling out details of the flood story. What does that say about the nature of the story?

4. *Literary genre of the flood account*. The type of literature represented in the flood story has been something of a puzzle. Is it a straightforward reporting of actual events, a story, a myth, a theological narrative, or (probably) some combination thereof? To that end, one could work on a variety of issues, from the repetition of key scenes and the details of the ark, from lists of people and animals, to the boarding of the ark (four times!), to the timing of the rains and the flooding, and even God's shutting the ark door. Structural issues have been surveyed, though the outline of the story is elusive and chiastic efforts have failed. Efforts to discern a pattern of sin, judgment, and mitigation have been common.[10] The turning point of the story in Genesis 8:1 seems especially important: God remembered Noah, his family, and the wild/domestic animals. This centering text shows that the attention of the text finally focuses on salvation rather than judgment, on what God does to preserve the creation beyond the disaster, climaxing in the story of the rainbow and God's unconditional promise. Does this mean that God the Savior preserves the creation from God the Judge? Or is God's saving of the creation possible only in and through judgment? But what, then, might it mean that God determines never to do this again? Not that judgment will never again be experienced, but that God sets limits on the nature and intensity of the natural disasters.

From another angle, the story contains little direct speech and no dialogue; Noah never speaks a word. There is minimal description of the disaster itself and no reaction from Noah and his family, with virtually no attention to the plight of the

---

10. See, e.g., Gerhard von Rad, *Genesis: A Commentary*, trans. John H. Marks, rev. ed., Old Testament Library (Philadelphia: Westminster, 1972).

victims or to their fearful response or to scenes of death and drowning—in contrast to the many horrific artistic renditions of the dying and forlorn that have been produced through the years. The difference of the flood story from the modern media's portrayal of disasters is striking indeed. Why is the text so reticent regarding the suffering of the victims, not least because the text claims that their own guilt has occasioned the disaster?

God and the Story of the Flood

A basic list of what God does in the Genesis flood story is remarkable: God expresses sorrow and regret; God judges but does not want to judge; God goes beyond justice and decides to save some, including animals; God commits to the future of a less-than-perfect world; God is open to change and is receptive to doing things in new ways in view of divine experience with the world; and God promises never to do this again. Even more, the story witnesses to a God who acts in judging and saving ways beyond the walls of the chosen community. Indeed, in the larger creational context in which the flood story is embedded, God engages in a remarkable string of activities that the chosen community has often reserved for itself. God elects, reveals, saves from danger and death, and makes promises. And this long before Abraham! And the biblical story suggests long since Abraham. From the perspective of many a Bible reader, these are problematic images for God—and commentators often move past them too quickly. Some of these convictions that I detail make us all a little uncomfortable theologically, or perhaps very uncomfortable. But I would like to invite readers to consider them and to think about how your own theological perspective might be shaped in light of them.

I outline these materials in terms of two basic considerations: the judgment of God and the recharacterization of God.

47

The Flood and the Judgment of God

It is common to claim that the God of the Bible punishes people for what they do (or don't do), especially the God of the Old Testament. Indeed, in many Bible translations we at times encounter the word "punish" with God as subject (e.g., the NRSV in Exod. 20:5, "punishing children for the iniquity of parents"). Is this a correct translation and understanding of divine action? In what follows I will claim that "judgment" language is more appropriate.

What does the divine judgment entail? First of all, Bible readers should note that God does "judge" (*shafat*) individuals and peoples in both the Old Testament and the New Testament; indeed, God is called "the judge of the earth" (Ps. 94:2; see Pss. 96:13; 98:9; Acts 10:42). Generally speaking, judgment has reference to God's ruling the world in an equitable way. As such, judgment may mean good news or bad news—against the wicked (Ps. 94:2; Rom. 2:2–9) or deliverance of the poor and needy from oppression by such wicked people (Ps. 76:9). But what does God's judgment entail? The use of this language for God commonly suggests to readers that God, like a human judge, sits behind a divine bench and hands out penalties or punishments for crimes committed.

But is God as judge best understood in such a way? As with all metaphors for God, the use of the metaphor "judge" carries with it lots of "No," that is, ways in which this language is *unlike* God. This is the case in at least three ways. (1) God's judgment is never simply justice. In terms of straightforward legal thinking, God is much too lenient or merciful. God is patient and "slow to anger" and open to changing the divine mind (see Jon. 3:8–10; 4:2). (2) Judgment is understood in relational terms; a relationship is at stake, not an agreement or a contract or a set of rules. This personal/relational dimension of judgment, not unlike the relationship between parent and child, sharply qualifies any strictly legal or juridical understandings. (3) God is not at all a neutral party in these

48

matters or an objective representative of an independent court of justice (such as a typical judge would be). Again, God is more like a parent, openly anguished over what to do about a wayward child (e.g., Hosea 6:4, "What shall I do with you?" and 11:1–9). What would courtrooms be like if judges were to display such personal anguish and anger? To mix metaphors: if God is viewed as the divine judge behind the bench, remember that God is also the spouse of the accused one in the dock! Objectivity or neutrality goes out the door!

The biblical language for judgment pushes in a different direction; it refers to the *effects* of human sin, not a penalty or punishment that God pronounces on the situation or "sends" on the perpetrators. That sins have effects is testimony to the way in which God made the world: human deeds have effects, for good or for ill. This reality is often called the created moral order: a complex, loose causal weave of act and consequence. The basic purpose of the moral order is so that sin and evil not go unchecked and so that God's good order of creation can be maintained and, if necessary, reestablished. *That* human sins, including the sins of violence, have consequences, including violence (see Gen. 6:11–13), is testimony to a functioning of the moral order, and this reality can be named the "judgment" of God.

Just how God relates to the movement from sin to consequence is difficult to sort out, not least because the Old Testament does not speak with one voice about the matter.[11] But generally speaking, the relationship between sin and consequence is conceived more in intrinsic terms than forensic terms: consequences grow out of the deed itself rather than being a penalty imposed from without. The evidence for this

11. For a recent effort, see Gene Tucker, "Sin and 'Judgment' in the Prophets," in *Problems in Biblical Theology: Essays in Honor of Rolf Knierim,* ed. H. Sun et al. (Grand Rapids: Eerdmans, 1997), 373–88. Tucker delineates several formulations: texts that are "dynamistic" and have no explicit reference to God (e.g., Isa. 3:9–11; Hosea 10:13–15); those in which God makes the connection between sin and consequence (e.g., Jer. 6:19; 21:14); and, least common, those that have a juridical element (e.g., Amos 4:1–3).

point of view is that several key Hebrew words for wickedness (e.g., *ra'ah*) are the same as those used for its effects (e.g., disaster). And so, such disastrous effects are "the fruit of their schemes" (Jer. 6:19; 17:10; Hosea 10:13). Like fruit, the consequence grows out of (or is intrinsic to) the deed. Ezekiel 7:27 puts it this way: "According to their own judgments I [God] will judge them." Many everyday expressions make a comparable point: you reap what you sow (Num. 32:23; Prov. 22:8; Gal. 6:7); what goes around comes around; let them stew in their own juices; your sins will find you out.[12]

Interpreters have used several different formulations as to just how God is involved: God midwifes, facilitates, sees to, puts in force, mediates, or completes the connection between sin and consequence. Ezekiel 22:31 makes the point well: God declares: "I have consumed them with the fire of my wrath." What that entails is immediately stated: "I have returned [*natan*] their conduct upon their heads."[13] In some contexts God seems to be more active in this process; at other times God takes a more passive role, such as "giving people up" to these effects (e.g., Ps. 81:11–12; Rom. 1:24, 26, 28). But again, this divine "giving up" is giving the people over to the consequences of their own choices, a reality that God has built into the very structures of creation. In the flood story, creaturely violence leads to an experience of cosmic violence.

The word translated "punish" (in the NRSV and some other translations) is commonly a Hebrew word (*paqad*) meaning "to visit." But the word should be more literally translated as it commonly has been (as NRSV does in Exod. 34:7, "visiting the iniquity of the parents upon the children"). Yet translations such as Jeremiah 21:14 (NRSV) often prevail:

---

12. Sometimes God as subject stands in a prominent position (e.g., Jer. 19:7–9); in other texts, God's stance is more passive (e.g., Hosea 4:1–3), even withdrawing (Isa. 64:6–7).

13. There are over fifty such texts in the Old Testament that link wrath with such formulations (e.g., Ps. 7:12–16; Isa. 59:17–18; 64:5–9; Jer. 6:11, 19; 7:18–20; 21:12–14; 44:7–8; 50:24–25; Lam. 3:64–66).

"I will punish you according to the fruit of your doings," when a more literal translation would read: "I will visit upon you the fruit of your doings." I agree with Gerhard von Rad that it is questionable whether the word "punish" is the appropriate translation for any Hebrew word in the Old Testament.[14]

This issue is made more complex by the fact that this created moral order does not function in any mechanistic, precise, or inevitable way; it is not a tight causal weave. Using the metaphor of cloth, the moral order is more like burlap than it is like silk. And so it may be that the wicked will prosper for a time (see Jer. 12:1) and the innocent will suffer because of the sins of others or for other reasons, often unknown. Ecclesiastes 9:11 even introduces an element of chance or randomness in relating deeds to their effects: "Time and chance happen to them all." In this discussion we also need to remember Jesus' own saying in Matthew 5:45: the sun rises on both the evil and the good, and the rain falls on the just and the unjust. Therefore, one cannot conclude that an experience of violence is inevitably due to that person's sin.[15]

The issue is made even more complex by still another reality: judgment is most commonly understood in communal terms. The fall of Jerusalem to the Babylonians is not unlike the judgment passed on Hitler's Germany by the Allied Armies; it makes no clean distinction between the righteous and the wicked. The effects of human sin ripple out and affect everyone in the neighborhood. That the innocent (e.g., children) are affected as much as the wicked is the issue that Abraham brings before God in the case of Sodom and Gomor-

14. See the formulation of Gerhard von Rad regarding Israel's "synthetic view of life" and Israel's lack of punishment language in *Old Testament Theology* (New York: Harper & Row, 1962), 1:265, 385. The practical implications of the translation of *paqad* can be seen in a comparison of RSV and NRSV in Exod. 20:5b. The RSV translates "visiting the iniquity of the fathers upon the children"; the NRSV, however, changes that to read, "punishing children for the iniquity of parents." Strangely, the NRSV translates the same formulation in Exod. 34:7 as "visiting the iniquity of the parents upon the children."

15. See chap. 3, on Job.

rah, another natural disaster (Gen. 18:22–33): "Shall not the Judge of all the earth do what is just?" And the children may suffer deeply.[16] Basically, in the divine response, though that may not be precisely fair, this is the way communal judgment works in an interconnected world such as the one in which we live.[17] Again and again, in many world situations, this lack of a clean distinction will prevail. And as we have recognized, nonhuman creatures will also be caught up in such effects. The effects of sin will negatively affect all related creatures; that is named as God's judgment.

Although the flood is understood to be the judgment of God, that reality is not presented as arbitrary or capricious.[18] Genesis 6:11–13 states clearly that violence, the violence of "all flesh," is the reason for the disaster.[19] The words "only," "every," and "continually" in 6:5 specify the depth and breadth of the sinful *human* condition. "There is nothing hasty, ill-considered or vengeful about God's decision; though God is far from being coolly dispassionate about the situation."[20]

16. For a treatment of the story of Sodom and Gomorrah as a natural disaster, see Terence E. Fretheim, "Divine Judgment and the Warming of the World: An Old Testament Perspective," in *God, Evil, and Suffering: Essays in Honor of Paul R. Sponheim*, ed. Terence E. Fretheim and Curtis L. Thompson, Word & World Supplement Series 4 (St. Paul: Word & World, Luther Seminary, 2000), 21–32.

17. For a thorough discussion of this issue in Gen. 18–19, see Terence E. Fretheim, *Abraham: Trials of Family and Faith* (Columbia: University of South Carolina Press, 2007), 80–89.

18. For an earlier expression of these matters, especially in the Prophets, see Terence E. Fretheim, *God and World in the Old Testament: A Relational Theology of Creation* (Nashville: Abingdon, 2005), 163–65. In the ancient Near Eastern flood stories, the motivation for the flood is not judgment on moral evil, but factors such as the teeming, out-of-control masses that disturb the world of the gods.

19. The phrase "all flesh" includes animals (Gen. 6:19; 7:15–16; 8:17), not least in view of 9:5, where animals are held accountable for taking the life of another; perhaps this is a reference to carnivores, the eating of blood, as a violation of a vegetarian way of life. This text is, then, testimony not only to moral evil but also to what is often called "natural evil." That is, the violent activity of the nonhuman world has ill effects on the earth's population. Also, see the promises given to the animals in 9:8–17.

20. David Clines, "Theology of the Flood Narrative," in *On the Way to the Postmodern: Old Testament Essays, 1967–1998* (Sheffield: Sheffield Academic Press, 1998), 2:512.

The divine motivation for judgment is made very clear indeed. Notably, sociomoral evil is the focus of the divine motivation, not idolatry or other matters of worship. Violence is inhumanity to others, illustrated in the earlier stories of Cain and Lamech.

To at least some degree, God has chosen to be subject to this just order (see Abraham's question in Gen. 18:25), and this cannot be factored out: God lets the creatures have the freedom to be what God created them to be. At the same time, the looseness of the causal weave allows God to be at work in the system in some ways without violating or (temporarily) suspending it. In these terms, God is a genuine agent. At the same time, God in judgment always works in and through nondivine agents. We learn from a study of the prophets, such as Jeremiah, that God and God's agents (Babylon under Nebuchadnezzar) are often the subject of the same destructive verbs.[21] In Jeremiah 13:14, for example, God speaks: "I will dash one against another, parents and children together, says the LORD. I will not pity or spare or have compassion when I destroy them." In 21:7, however, "He [Nebuchadnezzar] shall strike them down with the edge of the sword; he shall not pity them or spare them or have compassion." Again and again, God's portrayal is conformed to the agents God uses. To read the flood story in comparable ways, God acts in and through the agents of storm and flood that actually do the destruction. The people's sin has incurred a significant level of negative fallout, or "collateral damage," given the interrelatedness of all creatures; God mediates those consequences.[22]

In sum, people's sin generates certain snowballing effects. At the same time, God is active in the interplay of human sinful actions and their effects, and third parties are used by

---

21. For a listing, see Terence E. Fretheim, *Jeremiah* (Macon, GA: Smyth & Helwys, 2002), 36.

22. The agency issues cannot be factored out with precision, but some helpful claims are made in various texts (e.g., Hosea 8:7; 10:13–15; 13:7–9, 16).

God as agents for that judgment (e.g., floodwaters, Babylon). Both divine and creaturely factors are interwoven to produce the judgmental result. In more modern terms, our own sin as well as the sins of our forebears presses in on us, but no less does the hand of God. For history is our judgment, and God enables history—carrying the world along, not in mechanistic ways, but with a personal attentiveness in view of a committed relationship. God's salvific will remains intact in everything, and God's gracious concern is always for the best, but in a given situation, the best that can be offered may be burning the chaff to fertilize the field for a new crop.[23]

Now, how does the flood story fall into this pattern? Several matters of translation and interpretation come together in thinking through this issue. The words for "corruption" and "destruction" (Gen. 6:11–13) are from the same root (*shht*). So *tishahet* (corruption; 6:11) leads to *mashhit* (destruction; 6:13). Destruction is intrinsically related to corruption: violence leads to violence. One might say that all flesh has "corrupted" and indeed "destroyed" its way on the earth (6:11–12). Creaturely violence has disastrous ecological effects, a major flood (Hosea 4:1–3 tells this kind of story well, without even referring to God). As with *ra'ah* (see Gen. 6:5), as noted above, the language refers to both the wicked deed and, at any point along a continuum, the consequences, commonly translated "disaster, calamity" (so also *'awon*, iniquity, as in 4:13). This verbal linkage makes it clear that the judgment experienced flows out of human wickedness, showing the appropriate functioning of the created moral order.

Notably, God does not need to introduce judgment into the situation; the destructive effects of violence were already springing forth from the human deed. The judgment then is not some punishment arbitrarily chosen by God but is understood in terms of natural consequence, intrinsically

23. See Terence E. Fretheim, *The Suffering of God: An Old Testament Perspective* (Philadelphia: Fortress, 1984), 77.

related to the sinful deed. And God is mediator of the order of creation. But God does not act specifically to trigger the destructive flood. Certainly God states that destruction will be forthcoming, that God will indeed bring a flood of waters onto the earth, but God is not said to be the one who starts things. Rather, "the flood of waters came on the earth" (Gen. 7:6), "the fountains of the great deep burst forth, and the windows of the heavens were opened" (7:11; see also 7:17–20, 24). Water and flood are the subjects of the verbs. The seeds of destruction are contained in the very nature of the situation, and God mediates those consequences. God becomes the actor of a specific natural event only in 8:1, where God makes a salvific move, making a wind blow over the face of the waters.

The Flood Story as a Recharacterization of God

What might the flood story tell us about God? When all is said and done, this conversation about the flood story's language for God will leave us with questions, but that in itself is an invitation to consult other texts and to engage in further reflection. These claims about God are laid out early in the biblical story. This at least means that, as with any good book, we are encouraged to use these claims as a lens through which to read the rest of the Bible and its talk about God, especially as related to nature's violence. That the flood story takes up so much textual space—over three chapters in Genesis, longer than the creation stories—has long bedeviled scholars. Might the very length of the story suggest the theological importance it was believed to have in the biblical witness about God?

The following ten points overlap with one another, but they deserve separate consideration; they do not stand or fall together nor are they of equal import.

1. *Relationships.* Basic to the understanding of the God of this story is that God has entered into a genuine relation-

ship with the world.[24] God does not remain aloof relative to what has happened and like some divine mechanic seek to fix the world from the outside. God personally involves the divine self in its brokenness and works on the situation from within (a move that Christians will understand as Christlike). This dimension of the text reveals a major Old Testament conviction: the centrality of relationality, within God, between God and world, and among the creatures. For the Old Testament, relationships are constitutive of life itself; all things are woven together in and through relationships. To live in such a relational world means at least that all creatures will be affected by every other creature. We are bound up with one another in such a way that each of us is involved in the plight of all of us (cf. the economic crisis of 2007–9). And God has chosen to be caught up in this spiderweb of relationships.

2. *Agents.* God uses agents in carrying out God's work in the world, including acts of judgment. It may be said that much, if not all, of the violence associated with God in the Bible is due to God's decision to use agents that are capable of violence. And God does not perfect agents before deciding to work in and through them; nor does God necessarily evaluate the work of the agents in positive terms. God's agents may exceed the divine mandate, going beyond anything that God intended (Zech. 1:15). Notably, God assumes a share of the responsibility associated with that violence and takes on a certain blame for using such agents (Jer. 42:10).

Three dimensions of this issue in the flood story are important to consider:

a. As noted, God acts in and through the agents of storm and flood that actually do the destruction. Water and flood are the subjects of the key verbs that occasion the disaster (Gen. 7:6, 10–12, 17–20, 24).

24. For an earlier treatment, see Fretheim, *God and World*, 79–83.

b. The created moral order (acts have consequences) is also an agent in and through which God works judgment. As recognized above, the same word is used to speak of human wickedness, the violence of "all flesh," and its effects on the *earth*.[25] The destructive agents are *intrinsically* related to human corruption and are *used* by God.[26] Violence leads to violence. In other terms, creaturely violence has disastrous environmental effects.

c. God's agents in this situation also include a "righteous" and "blameless" Noah (Gen. 6:9). He fulfills every divine command, and his obedient human activity is sharply responsible for the salvation of a remnant of human beings and animals. This story testifies that *not all post-sin behaviors are a betrayal of trust*. A fundamental goodness continues to characterize God's creation. God will continue to place confidence in human beings for carrying out their responsibility for the creation (9:1, 7), and they are still understood to be created in the image of God (so 9:6). Even in a sinful world, the obedience of righteous people can have positive effects on the future of the earth and its creatures.

3. *God's emotions*. To make a more general point: this text is testimony to the affectability of God. God is deeply and personally moved by what has happened to the relationship with humankind. God is herein revealed as one who is affected by creatures both human and nonhuman (not just humans and not just Israel); God is not removed and detached from that world, but genuinely engaged with it and affected by that engagement. Several of the following points particularize this.

25. See page 54 above.

26. As noted above, it is likely that floods per se are *not* the effect of human violence; such natural events are an integral part of the world that God created. Rather, it is the range and intensity of the flood that is understood to grow out of human violence.

4. *God's regret*. God repeatedly "regrets" (TNIV) that God created humankind in the first place (Gen. 6:6–7). God knows what might have been and profoundly desires that things had not come to this! Here the past of God, what might have been, seems to stand in disjunction with the present of God, what actually is, and the collision of past and present in God occasions a deep divine regret and accompanying suffering for God. This point may also be considered testimony to the temporality of God (see above), who has so deeply entered into the life of the world that past, present, and future are real for God.

5. *God's plans*. God's regret seems to assume that God did not know for sure that creatures would take this turn to evil (as also in Gen. 22:12; Deut. 8:2). This does not mean that God is not omniscient, though some definitions of omniscience might be threatened by this understanding. The claim is still available that God knows all there is to know, including all possibilities, but there is a future that is not yet available for knowing, even for God.[27] Such language challenges any position that God planned for the creation to take this course. The corruption that has happened to the creation is due most basically to creaturely activity, not divine activity. At the same time, God bears some responsibility for these developments by setting up the creation in such a way that it could go wrong and could have such devastating effects. God created the world good, not perfect.[28]

6. *Human resistance*. This regretful response of God assumes that humans have successfully resisted God's will for the creation. As such, this text is a witness to divine vulnerability in the unfolding creation. This is a God who takes risks, who makes the divine self vulnerable to the twists and turns

---

27. For detail, see Fretheim, *Suffering of God*, 45–59. In thinking about God's power, it is often said that it is illogical to ask "Can God make a rock so big that God cannot lift it?" Comparably regarding God's knowledge, it is illogical to ask "Can God know a future that is not yet there to know?"

28. See chap. 1, above.

58

of creational life, including human resistance. Speaking of the resistibility of God's will becomes a key for understanding many biblical texts that follow, not least the many passages that speak of divine anger. To those who resist such an understanding of God, one may ask: if God's will were never successfully resisted, why would God become angry?

7. *God's changes of strategy.* God's initial reference to blotting out human beings seemed to allow for no exceptions (Gen. 6:7), but God's pain and sorrow lead to a decision regarding Noah that changes that judgmental direction, with positive effects for "all flesh."[29] The idea that God changes the divine mind is a relatively common biblical theme (some forty texts).[30] At the same time, significantly, this is not a change in the character of God or the being of God or the promises of God, but a change in divine strategy. Moreover, only the language of change seems capable of describing God at the beginning of the flood story and God at the end of the story, who promises never to do this again. It is God who has changed between the beginning and end of the flood, not human beings (although there are fewer of them around!).

8. *God's grief.* More particularly, God grieves over what has happened to God's world (Gen. 6:6–7). The NIV says it well: God's "heart was filled with pain" (the same Hebrew word used for the "pain" of the man and the woman in 3:16–17). The basic character of the human heart in 6:5—"Every inclination of . . . their hearts was only evil continually"—is

---

29. God's action does not depend on Noah's character; nothing that Noah has done is said to prompt Noah's finding favor with God. Rather, the motivation for God's choice of Noah lies in the committed relationship God has with the world, evident in the divine grief and agony over the creation and the suffering God has to endure. Yet, after being chosen, Noah's subsequent faithfulness (Gen. 6:9) is not just a blip on the cosmic screen, somehow irrelevant to God. Noah's walking with God counts with God, but it is understood to be a (not inevitable) consequence of God's prior action.

30. For a detailed treatment of this topic, see Terence E. Fretheim, "The Repentance of God: A Key to Evaluating Old Testament God Talk," *Horizons in Biblical Theology* 10 (1988): 47–70.

set alongside the disappointed and sorrow-filled divine heart (6:6). While the external and more objective picture in this story is one of disastrous judgment, the internal, subjective image is that of divine grief. To observe the judgment talk in the prophets, grief is what the godward side of judgment and wrath always looks like.[31] For example, Jeremiah 9:10 (with footnote), "I will take up weeping and wailing for the mountains, and a lamentation for the pastures of the wilderness, because they are laid waste, so that no one passes through, and the lowing of the cattle is not heard; both the birds of the air and the animals have fled and are gone." This image of God weeping over the judgment that has deeply affected humans and animals alike is paralleled in the flood story. Such images seem best illumined as that of a grieving and pained parent, distressed over what has happened to the human race (see Gen. 6:5–7; cf. Ps. 78:40–41; Isa. 63:7–10).

That divine judgment and divine tears go together has considerable theological import. Without the references to divine tears, God would be much more removed and unmoved. Judgment accompanied by weeping, though still judgment, is different—in motivation and in the understanding of the relationship at stake. God's harsh words of judgment are not matched by an inner harshness. The strategy is to portray the kind of God with whom Israel, and indeed the world, has to do: a God for whom judgment is neither the first word nor the last. A word about such a God can be productive of hope. Although God may give the people up to the effects of their sinfulness, God does not finally give up on them. God's judgment is always in the service of the ultimate will of God to save.[32] To that end, God can use judgmental *effects* for a variety of positive purposes, such as refining, cleansing, insight, and discipline.

31. For detail, see Terence E. Fretheim, "Theological Reflections on the Wrath of God in the Old Testament," *Horizons in Biblical Theology* 24 (2002): 1–26.
32. See Terence E. Fretheim, "Will of God in the OT," *Anchor Bible Dictionary*, ed. David Noel Freedman (New York: Doubleday, 1992), 6:914–20.

The ethical implications of this understanding of God are considerable. If there were no *divine* judgment on sin/evil, then *human* judgment toward that which is oppressive and abusive would not carry the same weight. At the same time, if there were no sorrow associated with divine judgment, then human judgment would be given a freer range regarding harshness.

9. *God's suffering.* Inasmuch as human beings are said to be just as sinful after the flood as before it (cf. Gen. 6:5 with 8:21), pain will be an ongoing reality for God. Thus the flood did not end the reason for the divine suffering. Although not simply resigned to sin and evil, God decides to continue to live with such resisting creatures (not the response of your typical CEO!). This divine decision to go with a wicked world, come what may, means for God a *continuing* grieving of the heart. Indeed, the everlasting, unconditional promise to Noah and all flesh *necessitates* divine suffering; a pain-free future is not possible for God. In other terms, the future of the creation that now becomes possible is rooted in this divine willingness to bear ongoing pain and sorrow. God determines to take suffering of all creatures into God's own self and bear it there for the sake of the future of the world. In some sense, the world's future becomes dependent on this divine suffering. God's suffering, climaxing in the cross, over time proves to be very powerful; indeed, one might say that suffering is God's chief way of being powerful in the world.

10. *God's promises.* This divine move finally leads to God's promises never to engage in such a destructive act again, repeated in Genesis 8:20–22 and 9:8–17: "As long as all the days of the earth, seedtime and harvest, cold and heat, summer and winter, day and night shall not cease" (my trans.). Comparable divine promises also appear in Jeremiah 31:35–37 and 33:19–26. What do such promises mean for God? For God to promise not to do something ever again entails an eternal divine self-limitation regarding the exercise of both freedom and power with respect to related matters. God

thereby limits the divine options in dealing with evil in the life of the world.[33] And given the fact that God will be faithful and keep promises, does that not mean—and I hesitate here—that divine self-limitation yields real limitation for God? God is certainly capable of doing anything, but the certainty of God's faithfulness means that God cannot do so. For example, consider what marital faithfulness entails: the individuals involved *are capable of* infidelity, but they *cannot* do so and still be faithful.

Considering such divine faithfulness, does God thereby give up control? The language of "control" is commonly used these days, but "control" is such an ambiguous word. Which sense of the word is meant? Is it absolute control (entailing the loss of freedom), mind control (hardly), crowd control (I like that image), ultimate control (certainly)? Most seem to use the word in the sense of absolute control, and that is deeply unfortunate language. At this early point in the history of humankind, the route of world annihilation has been rejected by God as a divine possibility. Divine judgment there will be (e.g., Gen. 18–19), but it will be limited in scope.

This move on God's part also entails a limitation of divine freedom. God remains committed to the freedom of the creature; they will be allowed to be what they were created to be. And their exercise of freedom might well result in the end of their world. Sin and evil will be allowed to have their day, and God will work from *within* such a world to redeem it, not overpower it from without. In spite of what people do, God will remain faithful. These several characteristics of God seem to me to be fundamentally in tune with the biblical center about a God who is gracious and merciful, slow to anger, and abounding in steadfast love.

In sum, what God does here *recharacterizes* the divine relation to the world. God qualifies the workings of divine judgment and proceeds to promise an orderly cosmos for the

33. Unless God uses this means to bring the world to an end?

continuation of life. God will never do this again! Human beings have not been changed by the flood, but in view of God's experience with the world, God charts new directions in relating to that world. It is this *kind* of God that provides a basic lens through which we are invited to interpret the God who is presented in all the biblical texts that follow.

If the Old Testament God can be so characterized, might this help readers come to terms with other biblical texts that speak of violence, indeed of divine violence, not least that which is associated with natural disasters? What difference might it make if one reads these texts in and through those images wherein *God places a limit on what God can do about violence*? Indeed, does not such a recharacterized divine way with the world issue in even more violence? By promising not to bring a violent world to an end, does not God thereby open up that world to unending violence, whether generated by human beings or natural forces? From another angle, by loosening the divine control of the world (which the divine promise entails), God becomes even more closely associated with its violence, or at least its potential for violence. Might such understandings be important as we seek to articulate the divine association with natural disasters in the postflood world?[34]

Although this story does recharacterize the divine relationship to the world, it also makes clear that God is not simply resigned to evil or simply tolerant of human sin. God must find a new way to deal with the problem of sin and evil, including the problem of natural evil. That way is the way of suffering and death. And over time, God's suffering proves to be very powerful indeed. For God to decide to endure a wicked world, while continuing to open up the divine heart to that world, means that God's initially expressed grief is ongoing. God thus determines to take suffering into God's

34. See Terence E. Fretheim, "God and Violence in the Old Testament," *Word & World* 24 (2004): 18–28.

own self and bear it there for the sake of the future of the world. It is precisely this kind of God with whom readers have to do, and it is primarily the word of divine commitment to promises made that they need most to hear.

The flood story shows, among other things, that human wickedness can make many disasters worse. The world, however, is quite dynamic, unpredictable, random, and wild, and disasters and suffering may come because of that reality and not human evildoing, as in the story of Job.

3

Natural Disasters,
the Will of the Creator,
and the Suffering of Job

Often forgotten in the study of the book of Job is that one
key reason for Job's suffering is his experience of natural
disasters: windstorm, lightning and related fires, and disease
(see Job 1–2). It could even be said that natural disaster is
the center of the book's discussion about suffering. Job's
experience of such natural evil leads him, his friends, and
finally God to focus on issues related to the created order. I
here explore the book through the lens of natural disaster.
In sum, human suffering may occur in God's world because
of the way in which God has created the world.

I begin with a brief look at my analysis in chapter 1 regarding several key themes in the Genesis creation accounts. In
Genesis 1–2, creation is understood not as a finished product or a static state of affairs but as a dynamic situation in

which the future is open to a number of possibilities and in which God's engagement with creaturely activity is crucial for creational developments. God's creation is intended to go somewhere; built into the very structure of things is its potential of becoming something more or even something different. In the development of such a universe, God chooses to involve that which is other than God, from human beings to earthquakes, tsunamis, periodic extinction of species (over 90 percent to our point in time), volcanic eruptions, and storms galore. All of these creatures of God participate with God in the continuing creation of the universe. It may be said that natural disasters are a key agent of God in the continuing creation of the world.

Suffering is an inevitable dimension of life in such a developing world, for both human beings and animals.[1] It is tempting to claim that anything occasioning such suffering is due to the fall into sin or to ongoing human sin. But such a perspective is much too anthropocentric a point a view—as if, for example, galactic explosions were the effect of human sin![2] The book of Job will argue that the efforts of Job's friends to link his sufferings with his sin are fundamentally mistaken. Job himself will make the sin-suffering argument yet maintain that his friends are mistaken in making such a link in his case. The book of Job explores various factors related to his suffering and will finally emerge with the viewpoint that his experience of suffering has to do with the nature of God's creation.

Creatures are certainly dependent on God for their creation and life. At the same time, God has chosen to establish an *interdependent* relationship with them with respect to both originating and continuing creation. God's approach to creation is communal and relational; in the wake of God's

1. See chap. 4, on suffering.
2. For human suffering as an integral dimension of the world that God created apart from sin, see Douglas John Hall, *God and Human Suffering* (Minneapolis: Augsburg, 1986). Hall, however, does not discuss issues of natural evil.

initiating activity, God works from within the world rather than on the world from without. And it is that divine decision, for the sake of a very good world, that will occasion much suffering.

I recall four ways in which Genesis 1–2 can help us think this matter through.

1. *God uses already-existing matter in creating.* The images of Genesis 1–2 bring God, raw material, and movement together and signal a dynamic rather than a static sense to creation, an open process rather than one tightly controlled. For example, the spirit of God moves over the face of the waters. Or God assumes human form (see 3:8) and shapes the ground into a human being (2:7). Or God creates the woman out of the rib (or side) of the man. Human beings (and other creatures) are brought into being out of already-existing creatures. God here creates out of something.

2. *God calls upon already-existing creatures to bring about new creations.* For example, in Genesis 1:11–13, God invites, "Let the earth put forth," and, as we are told, "The *earth* brought forth." The earth is a coparticipant with God in creation (see 1:20, 24) at God's explicit invitation. That story of the creation has been repeated over the millennia as ever-new creatures have come into being, mediated by existing creatures. Indeed, much of the beauty of creation, from majestic mountains to luxuriant river valleys, is the product of God's interdependent way of creating.

3. *God invites the divine council to participate in the creation of the human.* This interdependent way of creating is extended in Genesis 1:26, "Let us make," with God's involving the divine council. God here *creates communally.* The creation of the human community is the result of a dialogical rather than a monological act. Only social and relational human beings truly cor-

67

respond to such a God, which is the heart of what it means to be created in the image of God.

4. *God involves the human in still-further acts of creation.* The word "God" in Genesis 1 primarily has reference to God as one who creates. It follows that those created in the image of such a God are most fundamentally creative beings. As we have seen, this human creativity is illumined by Genesis 1:28; 2:5, 15, 18–20; and 4:1. Human beings are given a crucial role in enabling the creation to become what God intends.

Genesis 1–2 and Job

How might the book of Job be interpreted in view of this understanding of creation in Genesis 1–2?[3] I begin with some introductory comments on the book of Job. Most scholars understand that the story of Job, while probably reflecting deep experiences of suffering, is not a biographical or historical account. Job is "once upon a time" literature, a didactic tale, set in an unidentifiable place called Uz (1:1). In other words, Job is a "what if?" book, a "let's suppose for the sake of argument" book.

It would follow from such a perspective that the wager between God and "the satan" should not be taken in any historical sense either. It has been called "dramatic fiction." Readers are not being given a report of a divine-satan transaction that could have been caught on some heavenly recording. The book of Job is a story designed to pose key questions about suffering, presenting various points of view (the prologue,

3. For a bibliography of major studies on the book of Job and for a preliminary discussion of this interpretation of Job, see Terence E. Fretheim, *God and World in the Old Testament: A Relational Theology of Creation* (Nashville: Abingdon, 2005), 219–47, where I speak of Job's "strong emphasis on natural evil" (226). A more recent study of importance is that of Kathryn Schifferdecker, *Out of the Whirlwind: Creation Theology in the Book of Job* (Cambridge, MA: Harvard University Press, 2008).

Job, the friends of Job, God). These perspectives are offered to the reader as possible ways in which Job's suffering can be interpreted. That the reader is being asked to evaluate these varying perspectives regarding suffering is especially evident in the viewpoint offered by the friends. At the book's end, God explicitly evaluates their point of view in negative terms (Job 42:7–8). This divine evaluation raises questions about other points of view presented in the book. We are invited to follow God's example in evaluating what we read. A basic question is to be addressed: Which of the various points of view about suffering is/are being commended to readers by the author of the book?

From another perspective, the book of Job is an example of creation theology; neither Israel nor God's redemptive activity is mentioned. One of the more-startling points in the book is that creation theology may be a key resource for people who are suffering, especially those who are suffering from the effects of natural disasters and related events. We examine the major segments of the book in turn.

The Prologue (Job 1–2)

Certain aspects of the prologue have been shown by Job scholars, such as Norman Habel and Carol Newsom, to be "deliberately provocative," even "outrageous."[4] For example, God sets up Job for suffering by bragging about him to the satan (a figure in the divine assembly, not the later devil), and God makes a bet with him that Job will remain faithful even though inflicted with suffering (Job 1:8–12; 2:3–7). And so God *allows* (1:12; 2:6; this is a key idea in the book as a whole) the satan to enable suffering to come upon Job, within limits, so that God can be proved right! The testing of

4. See Norman Habel, "In Defense of God the Sage," in *The Voice from the Whirlwind: Interpreting the Book of Job*, ed. Leo Perdue and W. Clark Gilpin (Nashville: Abingdon, 1992), 26; Carol Newsom, "The Book of Job," in *New Interpreter's Bible* (Nashville: Abingdon, 1996), 4:360.

Job's faithfulness (the language of "test" is not specifically used) is not for Job's sake, but for God's, so that God can win an argument with the satan. As such, Job is deeply affected by a heavenly dispute. Indeed, in 2:3 God admits to having been "incited" (!) by the satan to continue Job's suffering "to destroy him *for no reason*" (Job 2:3)!

This picture of God in the prologue is deliberately provocative, for readers both then and now. Does God make bets with heavenly creatures about the faithfulness of human beings? Does God provoke the destruction of children in order to win a wager? Can God be incited or manipulated and "for no reason"? This depiction of God is not paralleled elsewhere in the book of Job or, indeed, in the entire Bible. This lack of parallels is important in assessing the book.

What is the author's purpose in raising provocative questions like these in the minds of readers? One effect of this story for many readers, especially in more recent times, is an understanding that suffering is an arbitrary, indeed self-serving *divine* decision. The story brings the reader right into the mind of God—wow!—and states why people suffer. And many readers believe that to be the point of the book and, often, an interpretation of the "why" of suffering more generally: God sends suffering directly into the lives of individuals to test them. But such a perspective raises many questions. One important question is this: Does the prologue portray a point of view about suffering that is to be *negatively* evaluated by readers, who are to conclude that suffering does *not* have such origins?

Why is God presented in this way? One might ask whether the purpose of the prologue is to provide a teaching moment for righteous persons, such as Job, who think that they have been given some special divine protection from the potentially dangerous workings of the natural (and moral) order. They have not! Or might the prologue have its roots in an individual who has become disenchanted with the "answers" to suffering provided by the author's contemporaries (e.g., the righteous prosper and the wicked suffer), personified in Job's friends? Perhaps. In any case, for the author to develop such points, Job's suffering could not be viewed as consequences for sins he may have committed. Job, a man of exemplary piety, is plunged into the depths of suffering. Job is a person who does not fit the popular pattern.

Two other verses in the prologue invite such reflections. They are Job's confession of faith ("The LORD gave, and the LORD has taken away; blessed be the name of the LORD" [Job 1:21]) and Job's question in 2:10, "Shall we receive the good at the hand of God, and not receive the bad?" Recall that the author of Job presents readers with points of view on suffering to be evaluated (e.g., those of the friends of Job). In these two verses, readers are being asked to consider: What do you think of Job's claim that everything that happens, whether good or bad, comes from God? Is this point of view about suffering being commended by the author to readers?

Probably not, for several reasons. One reason is that this point of view is the same as that of his friends in the dialogue, and God evaluates their point of view negatively (42:7–8). A second reason is revealed in the differences between Job's two confessions.[5] The first is a declarative sentence, the second is a question; the first is a more personal confession than the second ("I" in 1:21; "we" in 2:10); the personal name "LORD" (Yahweh) in 1:21 becomes simply God in 2:10. A third reason: when the reader moves to Job 3:1, we are told that "Job cursed the day of his birth"; this suggests, at least, that Job disagrees with his own earlier statements. The change in his own personal interpretation also appears at the end of the book (42:5), where he seems to relegate his own point of view in the prologue as hearsay. So the words of Job in 1:21 and 2:10 likely represent Job's conventional piety, a point of

5. For details, see J. G. Janzen, *The Book of Job: A Commentary* (Atlanta: John Knox, 1987), 51–55.

view with which he had been reared and that surfaced in this time of suffering.

The prologue raises another question: what directly causes Job's suffering? Observe that Job does not take a direct hit from God. The more immediate sources of Job's suffering are primarily from elements in God's good creation, mediated by the satan: fire and lightning, windstorm, and disease (Job 1:13–19; 2:7). "Natural disaster" is common language for all these realities, even disease (e.g., a pandemic); the phrase "natural evil" is also used for the effects of such realities, though the word "evil" is somewhat problematic in that no moral issues are involved. This is not to say that nature itself is evil, but that the workings of nature can hurt people (and other creatures).

Some of Job's suffering is also caused by "moral evil," the evil that sinful people perpetrate on others. The marauding desert dwellers (Sabeans and Chaldeans), presented in almost animal-like terms (and originating from outside of Job's social arena), kill Job's servants and carry off his animals (Job 1:15, 17). Notably, the God speeches in Job 38–41 address themselves to both natural evil (most verses) and moral evil (40:10–14 and other scattered references); both are considered to be the causes of Job's suffering, and God addresses them directly. But the emphasis in the prologue and the God speeches is given to natural evil and to the nature of the created order that God has brought into being.[6]

Job's suffering experience and (see below) the God speeches in Job 38–41 reveal that God has created a world that, in allowing the creatures to be what they were created to be, is filled with potential dangers and the real possibilities of suffering.[7] I suggest that the satan figure, which disappears in the rest of the book (as does the wager), anticipates this understanding. The satan is essentially a symbolic figure

---

6. See the recent study of Schifferdecker, *Out of the Whirlwind*.

7. See chap. 4, on suffering.

used to portray the way in which God lets the creation work. In effect, God gives the satan *permission*—a kind of divine allowing, to let moral and natural evil loose on Job (see 1:12; 2:6).[8] This image is emblematic of a God who lets the creation be what it has the potential of being and becoming, including catching up creatures in the experience of great suffering.

God's involvement in Job's suffering is limited to permission; God is not a manager of the workings of the world (let alone a micromanager). This perspective is similar to the understanding of Sabbath in the creation account (Gen. 2:1–3); God rests, and the creation is allowed to be what it was created to be. A more symbolic interpretation is invited by the fact that the "outrageous" ideas of God noted above (e.g., one who makes bets) stand unparalleled in the Old Testament.

And so, are the natural disasters that Job experiences the will of the Creator God? Yes and no, depending on one's definition of the will of God. *That* natural disasters exist in God's creation is God's will for the becoming of the world. John Polkinghorne comments helpfully on this topic: "I do not believe that God specifically wills either the act of a murderer, or the incidence of a cancer. I believe that he *allows*, allows both to happen in a creation to which he has given the gift of being itself, . . . allowed to be other than God, released from tight divine control."[9] Job's friends believe that if one is suffering, it *must* be God's *specific* will, due to sins that Job has committed. Yet since natural disasters are a key cause of Job's suffering, and since the friends' point of view is negatively evaluated, the book suggests that natural

8. One could raise the issue whether the *satan* figure is a possible "explanation" for suffering that is being explored by the narrator, only to be rejected by its disappearance from the narrative.

9. John Polkinghorne, *Quarks, Chaos, and Christianity: Questions to Science and Religion* (New York: Crossroad, 1994), 46, emphasis added. From his larger context, one might add an earthquake. Polkinghorne does not speak of Job in this context.

disasters are, generally, not due to sin and its effects. Such suffering is due to being a part of a complex natural order that God has created. The God speeches, to which I turn below, make it clear that the creation is not as rigidly fixed as the friends claim or as chaotic as Job thinks. We must find our way between these two extremes in thinking about Job's suffering.

Observers may ask whether at least some natural disasters are directed by God at specific creatures at particular times and places (one thinks of certain interpretations of Hurricane Katrina and the city of New Orleans or of the earthquake in Haiti). Would this not be true of Job? He certainly seems to be one who is targeted. But in thinking about such a question, we are asked to remember the outrageous nature of the prologue and to evaluate such an interpretation in those terms. The reader might also ask whether one purpose of the prologue is to provide a teaching moment for interpreters who think that they have a right to link sinners to the onset and direction of specific natural disasters. And God's negative evaluation of such a perspective on the part of Job's friends comes into view.

The Dialogue (Job 3–27) and the Elihu Speeches (Job 32–37)

These extensive chapters again and again lift up matters of creation. Job sets the dialogue in chapter 3 in terms of creation, and creation becomes the most common and intense theme that occurs throughout, most explicitly in Job 3:3–9; 7:16–19; 9:4–24; 10:8–13; 12:13–25; 25:1–6; 26:5–14; and 36:24–37:24. Job is absolutely right in centering his words on creational matters. He appropriately understands that his suffering most fundamentally *does* have to do with issues regarding the nature of God's creation and God's continuing relationship to it. But Job faults God for not creating an order that functions in direct correspondence to human behaviors. *The most fundamental issue for Job is theological,* more specifically, *a certain theology of creation.* For Job, God's creation is out of whack; it is a disorderly place that cannot be truly counted on and that God does not carefully control in a way that God should. God's wisdom as a creator is admitted by Job, as is God's power, but God is faulted for using that creation arbitrarily against people like himself. God's creation is poorly designed: retribution does not function appropriately, justice is skewed, and creation is anarchic.

Creation is the primary issue in the dialogue between Job and his friends. I cite two examples. Eliphaz's response to Job (Job 4–5) portrays the creation as wonderfully and precisely ordered; contrary to what Job thinks, it can be counted on. In 25:1–6 and 26:5–14, Bildad lifts up the orderly design of God's creation; he is awed by it and submissive before it (25:4–6; 26:14). Job contests his friends' analysis in a drumbeat of responses, refusing to go along with their assessment of his situation. He lifts up the incongruity he sees between the exemplary ways in which he has lived his life and the way he has been treated by God and God's creation. Job brings his laments to a climax by building a case for his innocence and demanding that he be allowed to bring his case before God, with charges regarding the poor design and the inept administration of the created order (Job 29–31). Elihu, another "friend" of Job, tries to mediate the issues at stake (Job 32–37); his opinions resolve nothing, but creation theology has a remarkable place in his speeches (36:24–37:24), which thus appropriately introduce the God speeches.

The Speeches of God (Job 38–41)

In these speeches Job is shown an amazingly diverse and complex world of nature. God's approach to a suffering Job is not to take him to a counselor but to the zoo, or better, out to "where the wild things are." This is the reality that has occasioned Job's suffering. By appearing in the whirlwind, God discloses God's self to Job within the natural order of things. God thereby depicts creation as both good and wild, both ordered and disorderly. This characteristic of the speeches provides an important clue to the nature of God's response to Job in his suffering. Job's voiced concern about the functioning of God's creation is a basic reason why God responds with creation imagery and why that response is eminently appropriate for Job in his suffering (Job 38–41). It has often been asked: how can such a journey through the wilds of creation be of help to a person who is suffering? That question deserves special attention.

One of the more-common remarks made by Job commentators is that the God speeches in the book do not respond to issues that Job has raised or to his suffering situation. Indeed, scholars will often claim that God puts Job down and, in effect, dismisses his questions. I here suggest that interpreting the book of Job in view of an understanding of creation such as we have suggested will prompt a somewhat different interpretation of the God speeches and the God revealed therein. God does actually respond to the questions that Job raises and addresses his suffering in a helpful way. One of the keys to this direction of thought is to think in terms of natural disasters, a chief cause of Job's suffering.

Speaking more generally, the link between creation and suffering is evident in this statement from John Polkinghorne: "God no doubt could have snapped the divine fingers and brought into being a ready-made world. But God has done something cleverer than that; God has made a world in which creatures could make themselves. But such an approach to creation has a necessary cost; it has a shadow side."[10] Or, in terms I have used earlier, it becomes messy. This being the case, creaturely suffering is a lively possibility in God's

10. John Polkinghorne, "Quarks and Creation," interview by Krista Tippitt, *Speaking of Faith*, National Public Radio, May 29, 2008, http://www.airsla.org/speakfaith.asp.

creative design of a naturally developing world. Such a state of affairs is a reality apart from human sin, not least if one considers the suffering of animals. The book of Job will help us to develop such an understanding.

God appears to Job in the "whirlwind" (Job 38:1); that word could be translated with terms such as "tempest" or "storm" (for use of the Hebrew word, see Pss. 107:25; 148:8; Isa. 29:6; Jon. 1:4, 12). The "whirlwind" is not some gentle breeze: it is truly a prime example of nature's disorderly elements and can even be called a natural disaster. God discloses God's self to Job not only within the natural order of things, but also right in the midst of what has occasioned the problem for Job (and not in the more usual mode as a divine messenger). God's revelatory mode in the whirlwind explicitly connects with Job's voiced concern about an unruly creation. More generally, God reveals the divine self as the God of creation, not the God of Israel or the God of redemption or the God who intervenes to fix things.

As a medium of revelation, God's revelatory mode has two functions. On the one hand, the whirlwind is intended to convey insight into the nature of God's world. On the other hand, it conveys to Job the understanding that suffering may be an effect of living in such a world. From God's perspective, Job "darkens counsel" (Job 38:2): he has obscured God's design of the creation by what he has had to say about the natural order. At the same time, God's speaking to Job is punctuated by insights into the workings of that natural order for his benefit. So God's concern for Job in his suffering is expressed in significant part by an expansion of his knowledge about the way in which the world works and thus is eminently appropriate for his suffering situation. In speaking in the storm, God thereby makes the point that knowledge about God and human suffering is at least in part made available in and through considerations about such disorderly elements in creation. God's response is directly related to Job's questions.[11] That God responds as he does, in creational terms, is in *direct* response to Job's questions about his suffering. And it provides *some* "explanation" (not the best word) for his suffering. Human suffering may occur in God's world because of the way God's world has been created and the way in which God lets the creation be and become.

The choice of creational themes by Job, by the friends, and by God seems to be prompted especially by the fact that Job's experiences of suffering have been in significant part due to natural evil. In these speeches, God ranges widely over a remarkable assortment of matters having to do with zoology, meteorology, and cosmology. At the same time, God ventures into anthropology in several ways, not least in the verses about the wicked in Job 40:11–14. These references relate to Job's inability to control or undo the behaviors of people such as the Sabeans and the Chaldeans of the prologue.

One point of these speeches is that God's governance of the world is not all-controlling; one effect of that divine decision regarding governance is that human beings are not protected from the wiles of the wicked or the disorderly workings of the natural world. God allows these creatures to be what they were created to be, without ongoing divine management in spite of their potential danger. Faithful ones, indeed the most faithful of all (such as Job), are not kept safe from either natural or moral evil.[12] We might, like Job, wish for a different world, without risk and without suffering and with full protection, but this is the world we have, and we are called to enjoy its remarkable gifts, not just to make the best of it.

The first of the God speeches (Job 38:1–39:30) focuses on the design of God's good creation. Job has charged that God's

11. From a pastoral perspective, conversation with respect to the workings of the world can often be helpful in the wake of the experience of natural disaster or disease.

12. One of the reasons for the prologue's stress on Job's faithfulness lies precisely at this point: the workings of the natural order may adversely affect both the righteous and wicked. The rain falls on the just and the unjust (Matt. 5:45).

world is not working as it ought if people like him suffer at its hands. God's directive to Job, "Gird up your loins" (38:3; 40:7), calls Job to look more closely at what he has experienced, to examine the complexity of God's design of the creation and his own place within it. Thus, for example, while God has created boundaries for the sea (38:8–11), the sea can still be a dangerous place. And God lets that creation function as it was created to function without intervening to rescue either individuals or communities if, for example, the sea is stirred up.

The second of the God speeches (Job 40:6–41:34) continues the discussion. This speech focuses on two mysterious figures, Behemoth and Leviathan. Though scholars are not in agreement in their interpretation of these figures, it is likely that they are actual animals (such as the hippopotamus and the crocodile). At the same time, they have become more than that, not unlike the way in which the dragon has functioned in our culture. These creatures are created by God (40:15, 19; 41:33, "creature"); however strange they may be, they are God's good creatures, not evil (in the sense of moral evil or a cosmic dualism), but they are dangerous. These creatures, then, may be termed "chaos," though not because they are evil or hostile to human life. Once again, these creatures reveal how God's good creation is not neat and tidy. God's creation is of such a nature that human beings can be hurt by it; certainly they do not have the power to control all its creatures, animal or otherwise. Many of the world's creatures cannot be contained by human effort or fully understood.

At the same time, it is not helpful to suggest that these creatures are fully within divine control (cf. Job 40:10–14); God has set creational limits, but within those limits God's own decision is that the creatures are *allowed* to be what they are created to be. They constitute elements of God's good creation that are not neat and tidy, even for God, and human beings and other creatures can be hurt in just such a world. At the same time, God has deemed that kind of world to be a good world.

Three features of the God speeches reveal ideas that relate to the suffering of human beings in the kind of world that God has made:

1. Human Beings Are Finite

God's questions to Job reveal Job's finitude. Human beings are created with limits; Job should know this better than he does. He is finite at two primary levels. One, he does not fully understand the way in which the creation works; two, he does not have power to control the dynamic dimensions of creation. Human beings like Job suffer from the weather and diseases because they cannot fully understand them nor can they manage them. One might also say that the human body is finite, and the experience of disease and pain is a universal human reality.[13] Moreover, as we have observed, Job cannot govern the ways of the wicked in the world (see Job 40:10–14).

So both natural evil and moral evil happen in God's world in ways that move beyond human knowledge and ability to control. Such lack of knowledge and power means that human beings may be hurt by the becoming of the world. On the one hand, Job needs to be more alert to how his own finitude has contributed to his suffering, as has been the case with every person through the centuries. Thus a basic statement about human limits is being made here; ironically, such an understanding is crucial for coming to a fuller sense of how God's world works and how we may adversely be affected by it. On the other hand, it is possible for finite, human beings to gain an increased understanding of the creation, and this could have a positive effect on the range and intensity of the suffering.[14]

13. Pain, by the way, is often experienced as a real gift. See Gen. 3:16 and the "increase" of pain. See chap. 4 below, on suffering.
14. On how increased human knowledge of the creation, especially in the last two centuries or so, might be related to God's call for Job to "gird up his loins," see Fretheim, *God and World*, 243.

From another perspective, we need to distinguish between the consequences of sin and the effects of finitude. One will inevitably make mistakes because of finitude, but mistakes should not be confused with sins (though sin may intensify our mistakes and their effects). For example, if we suggest that before sin entered the world, human beings would never have been hurt by the dangers of God's world, that would insufficiently recognize the effects of finitude on human ways of being and doing.[15]

2. God Created a Dynamic World

We have identified the strong emphasis in Job 1–2 and in Job 38–41 on natural evil. The world that God created is not (and never has been) a risk-free place, and God has not provided danger-free zones for righteous people such as Job. Indeed, God has created a world that has significant, if limited, elements of disorderliness, which can adversely affect its inhabitants (both human and nonhuman). This disorder and randomness is an integral part of "the warp and woof of the cosmic fabric."[16] God's creation is a dynamic environment, with all sorts of turbulence in its becoming, and these events have the capacity to bring suffering to human beings (and animals).

In the God speeches we are given images of boundary, rule, and law (e.g., Job 38:4–11); this world proves to be a well-ordered and basically coherent world. Readers are also given images of care and nurture, especially for the animals, whose unmanaged freedom is celebrated (e.g., 39:1–30). At the same time (as noted above), images of wildness and strangeness and randomness are present, including the wild seas, wild animals, wild weather (rain, hail, ice, snow, lightning and related fires), the uncertainties of the night, and Behemoth and Leviathan—the inhabitants of an ancient Jurassic Park.

---

15. See chap. 4 below, on suffering.
16. Richard J. Clifford, *Creation Accounts in the Ancient Near East and in the Bible* (Washington, DC: Catholic Biblical Association, 1994), 185.

All of these creational realities, however majestic they may be, are potentially dangerous for human life and health. Attending to this dimension of God's speeches is absolutely crucial: it provides the fundamental context for God's response to Job's suffering, which has occurred significantly because of natural evil.

In other words, God's creation is filled with *good* creatures whose being what they are entails risks for human beings (and other creatures) quite apart from the effects of sin and questions of moral evil. And so, for Job, storms occasion the loss of his children (Job 1:18–19), lightning destroys his livestock and servants (1:16), and disease takes its toll on him (2:7–8). From our perspective, we would also include such forces as water (both life-giving and dangerous) and the law of gravity (essential for life but also sometimes catastrophic). Without such potentially dangerous dimensions of the natural order, there would be no human life.

For all the world's order and coherence, it is not a tightly woven system (despite what Job's friends claim it is and Job argues it should be), and it does not run like a machine; some randomness, play, ambiguity, disorder, and unpredictability characterize its complex life. The proverb of Ecclesiastes 9:11–12 would apply to this kind of world: "Again I saw that under the sun the race is not to the swift, nor the battle to the strong, nor bread to the wise, nor riches to the intelligent, nor favor to the skillful; but time and chance happen to them all." Chance is a factor to be reckoned with in the life of every creature, whether righteous or unrighteous, and its effects may be calamitous. "No one can anticipate the time of disaster . . . when it suddenly falls upon them" (9:12).

Job's claims regarding a world that has significant chaotic elements and does not function in a precisely ordered way are largely accurate (e.g., Job 12:1–25), but *how he interprets this disorderliness is faulty, for such a world is precisely the kind of world that God has intended.* Job's negative interpretation of that disorder needs to be challenged and recharacterized.

In effect, human suffering, even suffering such as Job's, may occur in a good, well-ordered, and reliable creation, because that world is not a risk-free world! God's directive to Job to "gird up" his loins (Job 38:3; 40:7) is a call for him to probe his experience of suffering more deeply *in terms of the complexity of God's design of the creation and his own place within it.* God's questions to Job demonstrate that in order to understand his personal suffering he must revise his evaluation of the nature of the creation and the way in which God chooses to work in and through it.

In sum, the world that God has created is in process, and one effect of that reality is that it is not a risk-free place for human beings or animals. There is much about God's creation, beautiful and wonder-filled as it is, that is potentially dangerous for human life and health. God has purposefully created it that way. And even though God has full knowledge of the world's harmful potential for its creatures, God did not provide danger-free zones for human beings, even for the righteous like Job. And that kind of risky world, for all the suffering that may result, is deemed necessary for it to be a good world. We will return to the question of why this may be so.

Because we, like Job, are a part of this interconnected and disorderly world, we may, like Job, get in the way of its workings and be hurt. We can certainly make things worse for ourselves—finitude again!—such as being insufficiently attuned to the workings of such a dynamic world. So we build homes on the slopes of Mount Saint Helens, on insufficiently secured coastal areas and floodplains, or on the edge of earth faults. Moreover, human sin can intensify those suffering possibilities, but no necessary relationship exists between human suffering and human sin.

John Polkinghorne's words are helpful in this context:

We tend to believe that if we had been in charge of creation we would have done it better. With a little more care about the details, we would have kept the beauty of sunsets, but eliminated germs like staph. The more we understand the processes of the world, however, the less likely does it seem that this would be possible. The created order looks like a package deal. Exactly the same biochemical processes that enable cells to mutate, making evolution possible, are those that enable cells to become cancerous and generate tumors. You can't have one without the other. In other words, the possibility of disease is not gratuitous; it's the necessary cost of life.[17]

3. God Uses Agents in the Creation of the World

In our discussion of the creation accounts (chap. 1, above), we have shown how God works in and through already-existing creatures to create ever-new creatures. In other words, God has chosen to use human and nonhuman agents in continuing to work creatively in the world.

God's working through agents is also characteristic of the God speeches in Job.[18] For example: "Who shut in the sea with doors . . . and prescribed bounds for it, and set bars and doors? . . . Have you seen the storehouses of the snow and hail? . . . Who has cut a channel for torrents of rain? . . . Do you know the ordinances of the heavens?" (Job 38:8–33). The common procreation images for birthing the world in Job 38 also assume agency. God has chosen to use nonhuman agents in continuing to work creatively in the world; given the nature of the agents, the process will inevitably be messy (see also 40:10–14 for human agents). God does not perfect the agents before working in and through them. Hence, God's effectiveness "in working in and through such instruments always has mixed results, and less than what would have happened if God had chosen to use power alone. Hence, as an example, force and violence are associated with God's work

17. Polkinghorne, *Quarks*, 45.
18. See Schifferdecker, *Out of the Whirlwind*, 78n45.

84

in the world, because, to a greater or lesser degree, they are characteristic of the means of those in and through whom the work is carried out."[19]

In saying that much suffering is creational, God shows that Job and his friends cannot simply relate to issues of suffering through the lens of human sinfulness and related issues of justice. Job cannot understand suffering properly without a more thoroughgoing understanding of the created order. And so God engages Job (and every reader) in the task of reaching a more fully and more appropriate understanding of the nature of the created order and challenges him in the task of continuing to live in such a world with equanimity. Moreover, God challenges Job to trust that God's design of the world, however dangerous, does manifest a concern for the life and well-being of all its creatures. If this is so, the God speeches, with all of their creational insights, are remarkably pertinent to this moment in Job's life. In terms of another discipline, God is revealed as making a brilliant move in pastoral counseling.

The "Why?" of Job's Suffering

The basic issue addressed in the book of Job is not whether Job's suffering is deserved or undeserved. The friends of Job think it is deserved, and Job thinks it is undeserved, but as the book will finally claim, that is to ask the wrong question; what Job has done (or not done) is not, finally, the issue at stake. Yet if the issue of "deserving" is not the appropriate question, then what about the question "why?"[20]

God does address the issue of "why?" at one level, though not so clearly at another level. If a reader thinks that the prologue is an actual reporting of heavenly reality, then one

19. Terence E. Fretheim, *The Suffering of God: An Old Testament Perspective* (Philadelphia: Fortress, 1984), 76.

20. Schifferdecker (*Out of the Whirlwind*, 126) does not think that the book addresses this question.

85

answer to the question "Why?" is that God makes bets, and on his best horses at that. Moving beyond such an interpretation, one clear response as to why Job is suffering is that God's created order has significant chaotic elements that carry much potential danger to human health. *And* God has chosen not to manage this world to make sure that no one is hurt by it. God will let the creatures be what they were created to be, and in their finitude, human beings will have to struggle to work with that reality.

On another level, it is not entirely clear why God created this kind of world. Several directions for thought may be suggested. It is often thought that only a world of some disorder and uncertainty could be productive of genuine life.[21] Such a creation is necessary if the creation would be other than a drab, ever-the-same world. Such a lively and messy creation (to use our images from Gen. 1–2) is necessary if there is to be novelty, surprise, and ever-new creative ventures on the part of both God and creatures.[22] And God will sustain such a world that is both ordered and open-ended (and therefore dangerous) because of its continuing *creative potential.* In the face of suffering, one might wish (with Job) that God would have created a different world or at least managed it differently. But the potential for human suffering is the cost of living in such a creative place.

A related and likely perspective suggests that a parallel to human freedom exists in the nonhuman world. Just as human beings are not puppets in the hands of God and can use their freedom for good or ill, so also God has given to the nonhuman world a form of freedom to develop as it was created to be, which has included complex processes such as evolution (at varying levels of complexity). In such an understanding of creational process, suffering may occur naturally and, actually, should be expected. John Polkinghorne speaks of the Lisbon

21. See chap. 4, on suffering.
22. See W. Sibley Towner, *Genesis*, Westminster Bible Companion (Louisville: Westminster John Knox, 2001), 21.

earthquake on Sunday morning, November 1, 1755, in which churches collapsed, killing fifty thousand people. About this event (and related events) he says, "God's will was that the elements of the Earth's crust should behave in accordance with their nature. In other words, they are allowed to be in their own way, just as we are allowed to be in ours." Suffering is the "inescapable cost of a creation allowed to be other than God, released from tight divine control, and permitted to be itself."[23] And in the wake of the being and becoming of such a world, suffering will often occur.

God's commitment to human freedom (and free process for the nonhuman world) means that God's relationship to this world is such that God no longer acts with complete freedom. God is committed to the structures of creation, to letting the creatures be what they were created to be. Instances of suffering are not a matter of divine arbitrariness, but rather occur because of a creation wherein God "makes his sun rise on the evil and on the good, and sends rain on the righteous and on the unrighteous" (Matt. 5:45). Neither Job nor his friends can view suffering in any straightforward way through the lens of justice (so Job) or the lens of human sinfulness (so the friends).

Yet the design issues raised by God are at least indirectly concerned about matters of justice. It rains on the just and the unjust; there is no morality to the way in which the law of gravity functions; and the range and severity of earthquakes, for example, is not related to personal or communal ethics. Legal categories and justice-oriented thinking are not adequate for thinking about this complex world or its suffering. God's creation is good, but in being what it was created to be (and become), it has the potential of adversely affecting human beings, quite apart from the state of their relationship with God.

At the same time, environmental considerations (among others) enter into the equation. Given the communal charac-

---

23. Polkinghorne, *Quarks*, 46–47.

ter of the cosmos—its basic interrelatedness—every creature will be touched by the movement of every other one. Thus, for example, human sin can negatively affect the workings of the natural environment, intensifying already-existing directions of "behavior." Or global warming occasioned by human behaviors may strengthen the workings of storms, making them even more dangerous to the life and health of human beings and animals.

Such a world that God describes in these speeches represents God's willed design, and Job should trust that God knows what God is doing in creating such a world. At the same time, God does not ignore Job's questions about such a world. God could have dismissed Job's queries outright and shut down the conversation in a hurry. Yet God chooses to respond at some length to the issues Job raises and gives Job room to respond, thereby demonstrating that the "why?" questions are worthy of consideration and, at least to some extent, can help human beings understand some reasons for suffering, reasons not necessarily related to sin. God may be said to have created a good world, but that world is not harmless. Job and we ourselves might wish that God had created a different kind of world, but we will never know if such a world would have been less dangerous.

The divine relationship to this kind of world is such that God no longer acts with complete freedom but from within a committed relationship to the structures of creation to which God will be faithful. Hence, unlike the provocations of the prologue, instances of suffering are not a matter of divine arbitrariness but of God's bringing into being the kind of creation of which we have spoken. The speeches reveal that God's well-ordered world does not have a tight causal weave (it is more like burlap than silk); there is room for ambiguity and randomness that may occasion suffering. To be told that God is responsible for creating the kind of world in which suffering can take place may provide a remarkable comfort. At the same time, the speeches speak of God's creation as having a basic stability and reliability, and so it can contribute to an orienting vision for a time when everything is flying apart and the center no longer holds.

There is a price, sometimes a horrendous price, that people may pay for living in such a world. But this is a price that God also pays, for God too will experience the suffering that the creatures undergo. God does not remain aloof, ensconced in some distant abode. God is not like a mechanic fixing a car. God enters deeply into our suffering; rather than control things from without, God works from within.[24] Rather than remain in heaven, above the storms of life, God has chosen to join Job in his suffering and seeks to bring healing from within. And notably, God recognizes that healing may well take significant and sustained levels of conversation and intellectual engagement with the whys and wherefores of life. Some words spoken in a time of suffering are more helpful than other words. The God speeches are comforting words to Job, helping him to see that God is ultimately responsible for creating and for still sustaining the kind of world in which his suffering is taking place.

In sum, to say that the creation is good is not to say that it is perfect, as we have seen; at the same time, to say that God's creation is not perfect is not to say that moral evil makes it imperfect. For Job to understand his suffering, then, would be to recognize that God neither created a world free from vulnerability nor provided risk-free zones for the pious to be kept free from any harm. And God has chosen not to manage such a world to make sure that no one suffers hurt; God will let the creatures be what they were created to be, with all of the potential for creaturely suffering. God has made this creational move for the sake of the fullest life pos-

24. Christians believe that this way of God with the world is most supremely revealed in Jesus Christ. Jesus' miracles were signs of a new world, not efforts to fix the present world. Jesus stilled a storm, but Jesus did not stop every storm or eliminate storms from the life of creation. Jesus healed a leper (and others), but Jesus did not eliminate leprosy. We've been working on these matters!

sible. At the same time, and this point is important, Job's perspective and that of his friends must be able to be openly and thoroughly voiced before such a divine response can be fully appreciated.

Job's Responses to God (Job 40:3–5; 42:1–6)

God's directive to Job to "gird up" his loins (Job 38:3; 40:7) is a call for him to probe his experience of suffering more deeply than he has, most fundamentally in terms of the complexity of God's design of the creation and his own place within it. God's questions demonstrate that, in spite of Job's insight that the issue between them centers around matters of creation, Job must revise his evaluation of the nature of the creation and the way in which God works in and through it.

Job's response to God's first speech is deeply self-effacing (Job 40:3–5). He declares himself a "nobody" (40:4, my trans.) and has nothing to say in response to God. It is likely that God is not satisfied with this kind of response, and so God proceeds with the second speech. Job's response to this speech (42:1–6) is difficult to interpret, especially verse 6. In the NRSV translation of verse 6 ("Therefore I despise myself, and repent in dust and ashes"), it sounds as though Job repents for what he has said. But the NRSV is now commonly considered to be problematic here (a revised NRSV will not read like this!), not least because it is highly unlikely that Job repents of any sin.[25] The word translated "repent" is not the usual word for repentance from sin. Rather, Job now turns away from his earlier convictions and sees God's creation more clearly than he ever had before. Then, in the epilogue of the book (42:7–17), God responds by restoring much of what Job has lost, though not everything: his firstborn children are

---

25. See Newsom, "Book of Job"; Terence E. Fretheim, "The Repentance of God: A Key to Evaluating Old Testament God Talk," *Horizons in Biblical Theology* 10 (1988): 47–70.

dead. The end of the book of Job is bittersweet. But Job is content to live in such a world.

Job and Questions

Finally, it should be emphasized that the book of Job is filled with questions, from both Job and God. The book, standing in the lament tradition (see, e.g., Ps. 13),[26] helps us see that human questions—even shrill and angry questions—are appropriate in a time of suffering. As with Job, God may respond to our questions with questions of God's own. Responding to questions with questions is here a divinely sanctioned pastoral move. These challenging questions from God are an invitation to Job (and readers) to seek even greater understanding about the world in which he lives. Human beings, finite as we are, do not have all the answers, but there is much more that can be learned about the world that God has made than we presently know. Such understandings may help us respond more fully to the whence and whither of suffering. God's efforts to enlighten Job more fully about the nature of the creation in which he lives are an important model of approach for all who think about suffering, especially suffering that is occasioned by natural disasters.

In the end, God is more honored by the impatient questions of Job than by the friends who place certain questions off-limits. Here Job gives voice to those who are afraid to raise unconventional questions or who may be shushed up by those who think it is not right to ask such pressing questions. Job gives voice to those who cannot find their voices in the midst of suffering. Rest and healing may come only when we have shared our questions with God and about God openly and forthrightly. When we have asked our questions, we may be able to hear more clearly God's response to us—

26. See chap. 5, on prayer.

whether with further questions or some other direction for our reflection. We may then be caught up into the whirl of the wisdom, strength, and infinite resourcefulness of God. And with such a God, comfort will indeed become available, even amid disaster.

4

Suffering and the God of the Old Testament

To this point in the book, suffering has been an integral part of the conversation. From the messy ways in which God has chosen to work with already-existing creatures in the becoming of the world, the devastating effects of the flood disaster, and the specific hardships that Job undergoes at the "hands" of such creational processes, suffering—both human suffering and animals' suffering—seems to be integral to the kind of world God has created. Such suffering may not be specifically planned by God, but is not suffering understood by God to be a virtually inevitable part of the becoming of such a beautiful world? At the same time, suffering is a reality that has its roots in factors other than natural disaster. And so this broader understanding of suffering is important to consider so that the suffering from natural disasters is given a broader context. In this chapter we take a closer look at the nature of suffering and its place in God's world.

Walk up to any person you know or don't know, and you can be certain that you have one thing in common: you have experienced suffering. And at some level almost everyone has experienced suffering because of natural disasters. In any community you would care to name, there is grief enough from such experiences to freeze the blood. Sometimes the suffering is very evident to all; at other times it is deeply hidden, and we manage to keep our composed facades in place. However much one or another of us has suffered deeply and profoundly, no individual or community has a corner on suffering. At the same time, the word "suffering" can, unfortunately, be "leveled" to refer to everything from a headache to the Holocaust, with few if any distinctions made with respect to severity and impact, whether social or personal. Some differences within the category of suffering are important to develop, and that is one thing I seek to do in this chapter.

Suffering is something we all wonder about, even though the questions are not always or specifically voiced. At the same time, questions about suffering are more pervasive than we might think, both within and without religious communities. The questions of those who experience suffering vary, but God is often the one to whom and about whom the questions about suffering are addressed, directly or indirectly. The title of a recent book by Bart Ehrman, *God's Problem*, correctly conveys the idea that suffering is not simply a human problem; it is also God's problem.[1] And, as I have claimed, suffering would be a problem for God even if sin had never entered the picture. But how one articulates that link between God and suffering is a major issue, and many such perspectives have a potentially negative effect on the church's witness to God.

1. Bart D. Ehrman, *God's Problem: How the Bible Fails to Answer Our Most Important Question—Why We Suffer* (New York: HarperCollins, 2008), may be noted as a way of lifting up certain questions that are circulating (even if his "solutions" leave something to be desired). He raises questions not only about suffering in itself but also more specifically about the less-than-compelling (in his interpretation) ways in which the Bible (both Old Testament and New) often deals with the issue of suffering.

People all too often assume that the suffering they are experiencing has *specifically* originated with God. One need only think of the various God questions that were asked in the wake of Hurricane Katrina (or other disasters). I state some of these questions in direct address so as to recognize their often deeply personal character and to link them to their biblical counterparts (see below).

Where is God? Why, God, has this happened to me/us? Why, God, did you allow this to happen, and let it continue to happen? The last-noted question is often asked with a very specific sense given to the word "let, allow" (unfortunately). *You*, God, have decided to let *me* suffer? And if you let this happen, God, is that finally different from an understanding that you caused it to happen, or that it is your will that I so suffer? Do you, God, send suffering for specific purposes in order to test me or teach me or discipline me? Why me, God? Haven't I been faithful? Has that faithfulness really made any difference to you, God, given the depth and breadth of suffering I have experienced?

The questions to God or about God in the wake of suffering often go on and on. Why does God's response to the experience of suffering and violence seem so capricious and so occasional? Is evil out of control for God too? To some degree? Perhaps not ultimately, but in the daily round of things it certainly seems like it. Even more, is not God responsible for evil in some sense? Did not God create a world where evil and suffering could happen? However much human beings and the natural order are responsible for evil and suffering, does not the very existence of suffering show that it is (also) God's problem? Did suffering emerge only in the wake of human sin, or was suffering a lively possibility even before sin appeared, given the good but not perfect world that God created?[2]

Suffering is God's problem from several perspectives, as we shall see, but the missional implications might initially

2. See chap. 1.

95

be recognized.[3] The ways in which religious communities commonly link God to the problem of suffering have had a remarkable capacity to turn people away from the faith. I think of the response of a member of the clergy to the death of a child: "Someday you will know what you did to cause this to happen." It is not uncommon for people to respond to such churchly ministrations in a time of suffering with words or actions such as these: "I will never set foot in a church again." Among those who stand both within and without the church, much church-caused scar tissue exists. The issues of suffering and evil, and the often-problematic images of God associated with such realities—these are some of the greatest barriers to the mission of the church in the world.[4]

In view of the many questions about suffering that have been raised over the centuries, a number of "explanations" have been suggested or implied by religious communities (or their members). Many people have internalized these responses, and they may announce them in just such suffering moments (this may be what Job does in Job 1:21).[5] While more-nuanced formulations than the following may be forthcoming, unqualified "explanations" (and that word is often used or implied) such as these are often voiced and have a powerful impact in the lives of individuals and communities:

- Suffering is the will of God.
- Suffering has been sent by God for a purpose.
- God could have prevented the suffering but chose not to do so.

3. I speak of the church here, though the issue is not limited to that religious community.

4. It has been shown that a significant percentage of issues regarding suffering that people bring to ministers is caused, or at least contributed to, by their unhelpful perceptions of God. M. E. Cavanagh, "The Perception of God in Pastoral Counseling," *Pastoral Psychology* 41, no. 9 (1992): 75–80.

5. See discussion of this verse in chap. 3, above.

- Suffering is specifically allowed by God, at least for a time.
- Suffering is God's judgment because of sins committed.
- Suffering is bad and to be avoided at all costs.
- To suffer is to bear the cross.

At the same time, such "explanations" circulating in a community may result in people being afraid to open up a conversation about suffering, or at least their own suffering. The concern may focus on issues of personal reputation or standing in their own community. For example, they may think that others will wonder about some sin they may have committed that led to their suffering so deeply (see the friends of Job). If they do speak, their words are often thought to reveal a hidden anguish about the issues, especially the God questions, and in many communities this is problematic ("Keep a stiff upper lip"; "God doesn't like whiners"; "Don't ask 'why?' questions about God"; "You are caring more for yourself than for others"; and so forth).

A biblically based entrance into this conversation could be pursued in and through the key questions that biblical characters often raise about God and God's anticipated or actual actions. One thinks of Abraham's challenge to God over the potential destruction of everyone in Sodom and Gomorrah: "Shall not the Judge of all the earth do what is just?" (Gen. 18:25). Or observe Moses' successful intercession on behalf of a calf-worshiping Israel, pleading with God, "Turn from your anger, and think better of the evil you intend against your people" (Exod. 32:12, my trans.; see Amos 7:1–6). Or after the angel of the Lord has told Gideon, "The LORD is with you, you mighty warrior," Gideon responds in remarkably modern words: "But sir, if the LORD is with us, why then has all this happened to us?" (Judg. 6:12–13). These kinds of narrative testimonies invite Bible readers to engage in similar

97

challenges regarding actual or potential human suffering and how God might be related to the experience.

Biblical perspectives can at least rule out several overarching "explanations," as I hope to show. To know of these perspectives can be pastorally and theologically helpful, though this knowledge does not eliminate the responsibility of discernment. Jesus' response to the question asked in John 9:2–3 could help to set a direction: " 'Rabbi, who sinned, this man or his parents that he was born blind?' Jesus answered, 'Neither this man nor his parents sinned.' " Jesus thereby addresses himself to the issue of causality and eliminates two specific possibilities (the sin of the blind man and his parents), though not addressing others.[6] In what follows, I will suggest that Old Testament texts also address the issue. Generally, I hope to show that the texts do not claim *all* suffering to be the will of God or *no* suffering to be the will of God. Or that *all* suffering is due to sin, or that *no* suffering is due to sin. Or that *all* suffering is bad and to be avoided at all costs, or that *no* suffering is bad. Nuance is the name of the game.

More generally, deism (the absence of God from involvement in the ongoing life of the world) seems not to be represented in the biblical writings. At the other extreme, a monism or a divine micromanagement of the life of the world seems rarely to be claimed, if at all. It might be objected, however, that certain biblical texts do make such a claim.[7] Are these

6. The translation of John 9:3–4a is a problem. For example, the NRSV adds words to the original (and omits the word *alla*), suggesting that God sent the blindness for a specific purpose. In contrast, my colleague, Craig Koester, translates this text in this way (note the comma after "him," rather than a period): "Neither this one nor his parents sinned, but in order that the works of God might be manifested in him, we must work the works of him who sent me while it is day." See Craig R. Koester, *Symbolism in the Fourth Gospel: Meaning, Mystery, Community*, 2nd ed. (Minneapolis: Fortress, 2003), 104–5. See also John C. Poirier, " 'Day and Night' and the Punctuation of John 9:3," *New Testament Studies* 42 (1996): 288–94.

7. Among the "divine pancausality" texts sometimes cited are Job 1:21; 2:10; Isa. 45:7; and Amos 3:6. On these types of texts, see Fredrik Lindstrom, *God and the Origin of Evil: A Contextual Analysis of Alleged Monistic Evidence in*

texts to be understood as biblical "explanations" of suffering or not? I take a brief look at two of these verses.

Regarding Job 1:21—"The LORD gave, and the LORD has taken away; blessed be the name of the LORD."[8] But in a suffering context, one who cites the Job text without qualification does not seriously consider the function of the various points of view in the book, from the prologue, to the friends of Job, Job himself, God, and the epilogue. Does the narrator commend every point of view in the book? We know from the epilogue that God evaluates the friends' point of view negatively (42:7–8). It is not likely that this statement in 1:21 is being commended either, not least because it is identical to the point of view of Job's friends (see Eliphaz in 5:18). Given that the prologue is commonly thought to be an "outrageous premise" or a "deliberate provocation," one is invited to ask whether the statement by Job should be viewed with some theological suspicion. Job's initial uncritical response is common for people in such situations, resorting to a conventional piety without careful theological reflection. Without going into detail, the author of Job most likely does not commend this statement from Job.

The text from Isaiah 45:7 has also been cited: "I form light and create darkness, I make weal [*shalom*] and create woe [*ra*]." Contrary to some perspectives, however, this text does not stand as a declaration about the entire creation, that every event is somehow to be ascribed to God. Here the "weal" and "woe" have to do with restoration and judgment *in history*, not least in view of the following verse (45:8), which speaks of God "creating" salvation; and 54:16, which speaks of God "creating" the destroyer (see also 47:11; light and darkness in 42:16 and 60:1–2). Isaiah 45:7 is likely a historical claim and

---

the *Old Testament* (Lund: Gleerup, 1983). On the basis of close exegetical work, Lindstrom claims that no monistic texts are to be found in the Old Testament. See also the helpful article that touches on some of these themes by Frederick J. Gaiser, " 'To Whom Then Will You Compare Me?' Agency in Second Isaiah," *Word & World* 19 (1999): 141–52.

8. See chap. 3 for fuller discussion.

points to God's historical activities of judgment and salvation (see the use of this same language in Jer. 29:10–11).[9]

The Importance of the "Why?" Questions

To speak of "explanations" regarding suffering is often thought to be a problematic direction for reflection. No "explanations" ("answers," "solutions") to the problem of suffering exist; suffering is a mysterious reality that cannot be fathomed. Hence, a common "resolution" is to counsel avoidance of such considerations altogether and simply live with the mystery of suffering and care for those who suffer. Yet, I would ask, is this a necessary choice? Are the only options available to us either "explanation" or "mystery"? Is there a middle ground between these options? Can the consideration of the causes of suffering be combined with a profound care for those who suffer? Indeed, might reflection about causal issues result in even greater concern for the other? Although the language of mystery is certainly appropriate to use, suffering is not simply mystery.

Faced with the realities of suffering and evil, Christians can say something, but they cannot say everything or even as much as they might like to say. They cannot "explain" suffering or "resolve" the problem of evil or provide "answers" to these issues or develop an airtight "theodicy." Such language is sometimes used to characterize (or even caricature) efforts to say something, often as a distraction from pursuing the questions or as a way of shutting down the conversation. In response, as I hope to show, the Bible does give its readers some room to speak between silence and "explanation," though it does not propose a single place to stand in that room, as if pastoral discernment were not needed. And as I have suggested in connection with God's response to Job's suffering, bringing the nature of the created order (including

9. For other such historical references, see Amos 3:6; Jer. 32:42; Deut. 32:39; 1 Sam. 2:6; Lam. 3:38.

natural disasters) into the conversation may be of real help in such pastoral moments.

Through the years, as a result of a common critique of reflections about "explanations," considerations regarding suffering are remarkably and commonly subdued or even discouraged in the various communities to which we belong: in families, among friends, and at our liturgical gatherings. At least on the surface of things! I want to claim that it is important, especially in view of the biblical witness, for these questions to be voiced and thoroughly considered, not least the questions relating to the causes of suffering. As shown below, we must use care in the way we consider and pursue these questions. And such questions must not be pursued for their own sake; the issue must be directed toward asking, What shall be done for those who suffer?

We should pursue these "Why?" questions for at least six reasons.

1. *Healing responses.* Insights may be gained and measures developed that have the potential to relieve suffering (e.g., research with respect to childhood illnesses). The "Why?" questions often lead to rigorous work on behalf of others, not least those who have not yet been born. To know the sources of suffering and to develop healing responses may effect real change on behalf of many present and future sufferers.

2. *Human causes.* We often do not realize the extent to which our own words and actions have caused the suffering, including the often-hidden suffering of the poor and the underprivileged. Ignoring or diminishing the "Why?" questions is often a remarkably easy way to escape from our own complicity in such matters. We need to be confronted more directly and more often with our known and unknown participation in the causes of suffering, and reflections on such questions can be helpful to that end.

3. *Community approach.* Such lively questioning may enable us to explore more openly our own suffering and that of others in *community settings* (see the biblical models below),

with the result that the wisdom and counsel of others can be drawn into a conversation that is all too often focused on our inner selves and our own experience of suffering. This approach could help move us away from a fear of what others may think of us (what sin was committed that led to such suffering?) or a fear of "the worst."

4. *Facing the questions.* We may be better prepared to work with the questions about suffering that come from persons of faith and, perhaps especially, from their detractors.[10] A dismissal or diminishment of the "Why?" questions may not actually reduce their impact on people's lives. Such an approach will often only drive the questions underground, where they can fester and emerge in ways that are harmful, perhaps even deadly, to individuals and communities. We should also make sure that the "Why?" questions are not being discouraged because of the challenge to traditional understandings of God they may represent.

5. *"Whither?" questions.* Such considerations may be of help to us in pursuing an even more important question: what are you going to do with your suffering and the sufferings of others? "Whence?" questions must finally move to "whither?" questions if we would be appropriately engaged in these issues, but the "whence?" needs careful attention for the "whither?" to take on flesh. And these questions may help us to chart a helpful vision into the future for those for whom the "why?" questions will just not go away.

6. *Confronting God.* An especially good and important reason to ask the "Why?" questions with respect to suffering is to be true to our biblical moorings. The biblical texts are filled with questions of "Why?" and "How long?" regarding both individual and communal suffering situations. Set deeply within the biblical tradition, these questions to God and about God are challenging indeed. Some examples of many that could be cited:

10. See Ehrman, *God's Problem.*

- "My God, my God, why have you forsaken me? Why are you so far from helping me, from the words of my groaning?" (Ps. 22:1; see Matt. 27:46)
- "Why [O Lord] do you hide your face? Why do you forget our affliction and oppression?" (Ps. 44:24)
- "Why [O LORD] is my pain unceasing, my wound incurable?" (Jer. 15:18)
- "Why [O LORD] have you forgotten us completely? Why have you forsaken us these many days?" (Lam. 5:20)

The Bible dares to confront God with such suffering questions and invites its readers into a conversation about the nature of that connection. Even Jesus voices the "Why?" question from the cross (Matt. 27:46; Mark 15:34).[11] Key figures such as Abraham, Moses, and Jeremiah sharply question God regarding such issues (e.g., Gen. 18:25; Exod. 32:11–14; Jer. 12:1–4), and in each case God responds and does so in ways that do not shut down the conversation. Job also confronts God with questions and challenges regarding his suffering situation (e.g., Job 23:1–7), and God evaluates Job's speaking as "right" (42:7).[12] The book of Job actually moves beyond the voicing of laments and questions amid suffering to struggle in more intellectual ways with the theological issues involved (so also Ecclesiastes and several Psalms, such as 49; 73). These biblical traditions invite their readers to engage in reflections on these matters with equal rigor, sharp probing, and intellectual integrity.

A God of Relationships

Fundamental to thinking about suffering from a biblical perspective is the belief in a God who is in genuine though

11. See chap. 5, on prayer. On the importance of biblical lament, see Walter Brueggemann, "The Costly Loss of Lament," *Journal for the Study of the Old Testament* 36 (1986): 57–71; Daniel J. Simundson, *Faith under Fire: Biblical Interpretations of Suffering* (Minneapolis: Augsburg, 1980).

12. See chap. 3, on Job.

asymmetrical relationship to the world. God's will for such a relationship with all creatures is grounded in the relational life of God: relationality is fundamental to God's own way of being and doing. Generally, God's relationship with the world is such that God is present on every occasion and active in every event, no matter how heroic or Hitlerian, and in every such moment, God is at work on behalf of the best possible future for all creation. That God is always and everywhere present, however, raises sharp issues regarding the nature and dynamics of the relationship, not least those related to suffering. The question of Judges 6:12–13 returns: "But sir, if the LORD is with us, why then has all this happened to us?" Many who ask the common question in the wake of disaster "Where was/is God?" seem to be more concerned with issues regarding the power of God than the presence of God. Those questions should be explored together.

Although the nature of the relationship between God and world cannot be factored out in any precise way, the biblical material witnesses to several directions of thought.[13] For example, God has freely entered into relationships in such a way that God is not the only one who has something important to say. Prayer, for example, is God's gift to human beings precisely for the sake of communication within relationship, not least in a time of suffering. Such human words bring new ingredients—will, energy, insight—into a situation in which God is at work, and thus God understands such realities as a genuine contribution to the shape of the future at stake (see Exod. 32:7–14).[14] What human beings have to say to God can make a difference in their own lives and the lives of others. What they *say* counts with God.

---

13. In all such understandings of the God-world relationship, it needs to be emphasized that the relationship is asymmetrical: God is God, and we are not. For a fuller treatment of God in relationship, see Terence E. Fretheim, *God and World in the Old Testament: A Relational Theology of Creation* (Nashville: Abingdon, 2005), 13–22.

14. See chap. 5 for further reflection on prayer.

For another example, and a key one for considering suffering, God has freely entered into relationships in such a way that God is not the only one who has something to do and the power with which to do it. The first words that God speaks to the newly created human beings (Gen. 1:28), in developing what "image of God" means, involves commands that entail the possession and use of creaturely power: be fruitful, multiply, fill the earth, subdue, have dominion. For the sake of a genuine relationship, God thereby freely chooses not to be the only one with power in the world, entrusting creatures in the use of their God-given powers. God moves over, as it were, and makes room for others to be what they are created to be. What they *do* counts with God.

This understanding of power in the God-human relationship is complicated by God's decision to place certain actions off-limits for God. Think of God's recurring promises in the Bible (e.g., Gen. 8:20–21; 9:8–17). What do such promises mean for God? For God to promise not to do something ever again entails a divine self-limitation regarding the exercise of both freedom and power. God thereby limits the divine options in dealing with evil in the life of the world. Certainly God is *capable* of doing anything, but the certainty of God's faithfulness means that God has limited the divine possibilities for action on any related issue.[15]

In honoring this basic character of the Creator-creature relationship, God chooses to use constraint and restraint in exercising power in the life of the world. This is a risky move for God. God may well look bad in the eyes of those who think that God should not exercise such constraint and should simply take charge or take control of such suffering moments in our lives. God's honoring of relationship opens God up to the charge of neglect. Yet, even in the face of human sinfulness and its suffering effects, God continues to entrust human beings with creaturely responsibilities and the power

15. For further discussion, see chaps. 1 and 2.

to carry them out (see Ps. 8). From another angle, such a divine commitment leaves God open to the charge of violence, for God may choose to act in and through agents who use violent means (e.g., the Babylonian armies).[16] God's efficacy in and through such less-than-perfect instruments will always have mixed results and be less in accord with God's good will than what would have happened if God had chosen to use power alone. The effects of a divine self-limitation in the exercise of power needs close attention in any consideration of the relationship between God and suffering.

Responses to the "Why?" of Suffering

Regarding the "Why?" or "Whence?" of suffering, the biblical material permits us to make several distinctions,[17] though without suggesting that every suffering experience can somehow be named or gathered in these terms. At the same time, as mentioned above, a possible discernment of the specific "Whence?" of an instance of suffering may be important in helping to shape the nature of the pastoral or theological or ethical response. Generally it is important to recognize suffering as having effects that are holistic, affecting bodily, social, psychical, and spiritual dimensions of our lives, and in interrelated ways. This reality is true of each of the categories of suffering described below.

Suffering as Part of God's Good Creation

As seen in an earlier chapter, God's world is not a suffering-free or pain-free world, and God created it that way. The fol-

16. A contemporary example could be God's use of the Allied Armies in World War II, armies that at times exceeded the divine mandate. For detail, see Terence E. Fretheim, " 'I Was Only a Little Angry': Divine Violence in the Prophets," *Interpretation* 58 (2004): 365–75.

17. I am indebted to Douglas John Hall, *God and Human Suffering: An Exercise in the Theology of the Cross* (Minneapolis: Augsburg, 1986), 53–67, for prompting this type of reflection.

lowing subpoints overlap in some ways, but distinctions may be helpful as we think the matter through from various angles.[18]

1. *Suffering and human limitation.* Human beings are created with limits—of intelligence, agility, speed, and strength—that lead to suffering in various forms. Douglas John Hall speaks of "Suffering as Becoming."[19] Suffering is a universal human reality; it goes with life as God has created it (apart from sin) and can serve God's purposes for the fullest life possible. Hall grounds this understanding in the biblical text, especially the opening chapters of Genesis and in the life of Jesus (see, e.g., Matt. 26:36–40; Heb. 5:7). Hall speaks of loneliness (Gen. 2:18, "It is not good that the man should be alone"); temptation (in considering alternatives); anxiety (associated with negative possibilities); finitude (limits of varying sorts).

From going to school and preparing for examinations, we know that struggle and challenge are necessary for personal growth and development. A pain-free life would be a lifeless life. To paraphrase D. J. Hall, "Life depends in some mysterious way on the struggle to be.... If nothing were inaccessible, nothing out of reach, and there were no unfulfilled dreams or wishes, there would also be no wonder, no surprise, and no gratitude."[20] If we stretch those limits (as in education or sports), we may suffer for the sake of gain. As the familiar proverb has it, "No pain, no gain." If such suffering serves life, it can be called good and counted as part of God's intentions for the creation. Or recall Genesis 3:16, where God announces that the woman in childbirth shall experience an "increase" in pain; this implies that pain (from a stretching of the body) was understood to be an integral part of childbirth; only now, in the wake of sin, that pain is intensified.

Or we may suffer because we make mistakes. If "Adam and Eve" (as pre-sin human beings) had taken examinations, they

18. Some of these items have surfaced in the discussion of Job (see chap. 3).
19. Hall, *God and Human Suffering,* 49–71.
20. Ibid., 60, 58. One might gather other forms of suffering due to finitude, such as suffering associated with change or loss or even death.

would not have earned a perfect score every time. When we test our mental limits, we may commit errors of judgment. Or when we test our bodily limits (as in climbing) we may suffer (as in a fall), not because we sin but because we make mistakes, or someone else does.

or we are too weak

Accidents can happen in the world that God created. God has not created a risk-free world; indeed, one can say that God created a dangerous world. At least the potential for suffering is real, and no little care is necessary if one would live in this world without being hurt or endangering one's life. For example, water is both gift and danger; the law of gravity is both gift and danger. If "Adam and Eve" had fallen and broken an arm or a leg, it would have hurt. Sin can intensify the risk (e.g., we may fall because we have been pushed), but it must be strongly affirmed that suffering has no necessary relationship to sin.[21] Even without sin, suffering would be an integral part of life. From another angle, one might say that the capacity to experience pain is a gift and part of God's good creation (think of getting one's hand too close to a fire).

2. Suffering and nature. As recognized in previous chapters, the world is also in the process of becoming. God has created a dynamic world; earthquakes, volcanoes, glaciers, storms, bacteria, and viruses have their role to play in the world's becoming. This is an orderly process in many ways, but it is also disorderly and messy. The potential for natural evil (ill effects on creatures from the functioning of the natural order) was present from the beginning. Indeed, one could even speak of violence as part of God's good creation (think of the animal world). Because we are part of this interconnected world, and our finitude comes into play, we may get in the way of these natural processes and be hurt by them. And God has not placed human beings in safe zones so that they might be protected from such a developing world. Sin,

---

21. See chap. 3, on Job.

however, can intensify the encounter and the associated suffering (e.g., recklessness in the operation of vehicles).

3. *Suffering due to God's allowing creatures to be themselves.* In another context, we have noticed the importance of God's resting on the Sabbath day (Gen. 2:1–3). God steps back from what has been created and "allows" the creatures to be and become what they were created to be, without divine management of their moves. The language of God's "allowing" (letting) is a common human response in the wake of a suffering experience. Such language, however, is often used in the sense that God *sent* a given experience of suffering, with a meaning no different from saying that God caused it. It is important, however, to distinguish between a *specific* allowing (where every creaturely move is controlled by God) and a *general* allowing, an approach that God takes to every creature at all times, honoring their particular creaturehood. In the words of John Polkinghorne, "The suffering and evil of the world are not due to weakness, oversight, or callousness on God's part, but, rather, they are the inescapable cost of a creation *allowed* to be other than God, released from tight divine control, and permitted to be itself."[22] The parent-child relationship comes to mind.

4. *Suffering and randomness.* Randomness also plays a role in the becoming of the world. This language is a mainstay of current scientific understandings of the way in which the world works, but it is already recognized in biblical times. In the words of Ecclesiastes 9:11, "Again I saw that under the sun the race is not to the swift, nor the battle to the strong, nor bread to the wise, nor riches to the intelligent, nor favor to the skillful; but time and chance happen to them all." In each of the cases listed, it would be natural to think that the swift and the strong always win, and the wise and intelligent and skillful always get it right, with consequent rewards for their labor.

22. John Polkinghorne, *Quarks, Chaos, and Christianity: Questions to Science and Religion* (New York: Crossroad, 1994), 47, emphasis added.

But we all know that life is not like that. One thinks of random encounters with certain storms or viruses or the randomness of the gene pool. (It has been said that there is no lifeguard at the gene pool!) Often the birth of a disabled child occasions an agonizing over what was done to "deserve" such a son or daughter. It is not unimportant to ask the "Why?" questions; for example, parents may have done something during the gestation period that occasioned such an effect (e.g., using alcohol). But it must be recognized that randomness remains an often-unrecognized factor in the issues of maternity/paternity; to know of this reality can be theologically and pastorally helpful.

Also included in the world that God created good are such matters as cell mutation, which are a necessary dimension of creaturely development but can also lead to suffering. The possibility of disease, for example, is an integral part of God's good creation. Even if there had been no sin, cancer and other diseases had the potential of developing in such a world.

5. Suffering and God's decision to use agents. Earlier in this volume we have seen that God chose to create the world in an interdependent way. This divine way of working in concert with creatures continues through the millennia: God chooses to work in and through agents to carry out God's work in the world. This divine decision signals a basic, foundational divine approach to working with the world. Once this divine way is recognized, then we are again (given the finitude of creatures and the sinfulness of human beings) introduced to a certain messiness in the way in which God accomplishes things in the world. Earlier we considered why God chose such a communal way of working in the world, deciding not do everything alone.[23] As a result, we recognize that God certainly bears some responsibility for the terrible things that can happen in and through the work of agents.

23. See above, 53–55, 84–85 (chaps. 2 and 3).

God does not perfect human beings and other agents, overcoming all of their foibles and flaws, before deciding to work with them and through them. God works with what is available, including the institutions of society. Again we see a certain messiness that results from this divine way of working. Among such institutions in that ancient Israelite context were certain ways of waging war and other trappings of government. More generally, violence is associated with God's work in the world because, to a greater or lesser degree, violence is characteristic of the persons, institutions, and other creatures through which that work of God is done.

And God does not (micro)manage the work of the agents but uses constraint and restraint in allowing them to exercise freedom. God's work in and through such agents will always have mixed results, will be less than what would have happened had God chosen to do everything all by God's self. Moreover, God does not necessarily confer a positive value on those means in and through which God works. At the same time, language used for the agent is often also used for God; the portrayal of God in the text is conformed to the agents that God uses (cf. Jer. 13:14 with. 21:7).[24]

God's agents may exceed the divine mandate and have actually done so again and again, going beyond anything that God had willed or intended. God assumes a share of the responsibility associated with that misuse and takes part of the blame for using such agents (see Jer. 42:10; Zech. 1:15).

Most basically, the created moral order is an agent of God. The "moral order" might be defined as a complex, loose causal weave of act and consequence. That sins have consequences, including suffering and violence, is ongoing testimony to the *proper* functioning of the moral order. This reality can be named the judgment of God. And so God, for

24. This link is very common. A modern parallel might be cited: God's work in the church is often associated with the work of agents like ourselves, and God's reputation suffers because God is thereby associated with an awful lot of, say, incompetence.

111

the sake of the world, institutes an order of things that has considerable potential to occasion suffering in the life of the world. To this we now turn.

Suffering as the Consequence of Sin and Evil

We know from experience and common sense that sin can cause suffering. In terms of the previous category, human sin can intensify and/or distort the suffering of becoming, so that it does not serve life (e.g., anxiety can become an anxiousness that is life-debilitating). But it is important to make a fundamental distinction between human suffering occasioned by an individual's (or communities') own sin and the suffering that is due to the sins of other people. This distinction is rooted in an important biblical perspective. Two key events in Israel's history frame this discussion. The exodus is a prime example of Israel's suffering because of what the Egyptians had done to them; the suffering of Israel in the destruction of Jerusalem and the exile is due to the people's own sin (see the book of Lamentations).

Presumably God could have created a world in which sins never had suffering consequences. But without consequences to our words and deeds, there would be no genuine moral choice, and human beings would not be morally responsible. Moreover, with no consequences, sin and evil would go unchecked in the life of the world. And it needs to be considered whether such a divine move would not have resulted in forms of suffering that are much worse than what we now know.

1. *Suffering as the consequence of our own sin.* Individual (and corporate) sins can cause suffering to those who commit them because God made a world in which actions have consequences for both individuals and communities. The Bible is filled with just such examples from its early chapters on (from, e.g., the sin of Adam and Eve in Gen. 3 to that of David with Bathsheba in 2 Sam. 12). In a more modern example, if you take drugs and drive your car into a ditch,

you may well suffer. We have several everyday phrases we use to describe this reality: what goes around comes around; chickens come home to roost.

The Bible often names these effects as divine judgment. But just how God relates to the movement from sinful act to consequence is difficult to sort out, not least because the Old Testament does not speak with one voice about the matter.[25] But generally speaking, the move from sin to consequence is conceived in intrinsic rather than forensic terms: consequences grow out of the deed itself rather than being imposed by God from without as a penalty. Thus God *sees to* the workings of the created moral order and mediates "the fruit of their schemes" (e.g., through the Babylonian armies [Jer. 6:19; 21:14] or authorities more generally [Rom. 13:4]).[26] As an example of the nature of God's involvement, see Ezekiel 22:31. God declares: "I have consumed them with the fire of my wrath." What that entails is immediately stated: "I have returned their conduct upon their heads." God does not (need to) introduce judgment into the situation; the destructive effects are already springing forth from the human deed.

So God, in creating such a moral order, introduces into the very workings of the world (act-consequence) considerable *potential* for suffering. And this responsibility of God should not be downplayed. But it is the actions of human beings that "trigger" such suffering consequences. And because such a functioning of the world is best for the world and its creatures, God will continue to see to (or mediate, facilitate, oversee) such a world. Hence, God as the subject of such verbs becomes associated with much suffering and violence.

At the same time, this act-consequence world in which we live does not run like a machine, with precise consequences that

---

25. For more detail, see chap. 2, on the flood story.

26. On the contingent character of divine wrath and judgment, see the excellent discussion of Abraham Heschel, *The Prophets* (San Francisco: Harper & Row, 1962), 279–98.

are predictable for certain actions. One thinks of Jeremiah's complaint to God (Jer. 12:1): "Why does the way of the guilty prosper? Why do all who are treacherous thrive?" From another angle, because of the looseness of the causal weave, many innocent people (e.g., children) get caught in its workings and suffer undeservedly (this is the concern of Abraham over the destruction of Sodom and Gomorrah; see Gen. 18:22–33). Sometimes people's sinful actions do not result in such suffering consequences, even though they often do, and some innocents do suffer. Such a looseness in the moral order strongly suggests that God does not manage it in some precise way.

These considerations also apply to the following category.

2. *Suffering as the consequence of the sins of other people.* We often experience suffering, not because of something we have done, but because of what others have done to us. One thinks of child abuse. The Israelites in Egypt suffered because of the harsh policies of the Egyptian leaders (see Exod. 1–2). Importantly, as one thinks of directions for response in other oppressive situations, God did not advise the Israelites to endure their suffering, but moved to get them out of that abusive situation, the results of which are called "salvation" (15:2). This understanding of salvation, with its sociopolitical dimensions, is often neglected in thinking of God's work.

God's deliverance of the Israelites entailed judgment against the Egyptians. So the ones causing the suffering came to experience a comparable suffering (at least). More generally, some of the sharpest indictments of human sinfulness and most forthright announcements of divine judgment are directed at those who abuse the less-fortunate neighbor, whether members of the chosen people or not (e.g., Exod. 22:21–28).[27] Many of the psalms have reference to suffering at the hands of others, such as Psalm 55, reflecting a situation

27. On issues of moral order, see Klaus Koch, "Is There a Doctrine of Retribution in the Old Testament?" in *Theodicy and the Old Testament*, ed. James L. Crenshaw (Philadelphia: Fortress, 1983), 57–87; Patrick Miller, *Sin and Judgment in the Prophets* (Chico, CA: Scholars Press, 1983).

of domestic abuse. It is striking that so many psalms of the innocent sufferer exist compared to the psalms of penitence (e.g., Ps. 51).[28]

3. *Moral order affects cosmic order.* God created an interrelated world, in which the actions (indeed, the very presence) of one creature can affect the "life" of other creatures for good or for ill. So, for example, human sin may have a negative effect on the becoming of creation (e.g., the suffering of animals). The natural order may take a course that is distorted from what would have been the case apart from human sin. One thinks of environmental devastation. The Bible recognizes this link in passages such as Hosea 4:1–3: "Hear the word of the LORD, O people of Israel . . . Swearing, lying, and murder, and stealing and adultery break out; bloodshed follows bloodshed. Therefore the land mourns, and all who live in it languish, together with the wild animals and the birds of the air, even the fish of the sea are perishing." Human sin can have devastating effects on the natural world around us. On the other hand, human activity may contribute to the good development of the larger world around us (e.g., care for the land or the animals).

Suffering as the Tragic Effects of Sin over Time

We also suffer because we belong to communities that have had a long history of sinfulness and are saturated with its effects. The common result is that the effects of sin, which can be named "evil," take on a life of their own and become integrated into the very structures of our life together, in family, community, congregation, nation, and world. Suffering and its effects have become pervasive and woven into the fabric of life. They become part of "the system" that each generation inherits. This is manifested in such realities as ageism, racism, classism, sexism, and plain old dysfunctionality.

28. See chap. 5, on prayer.

Everyone will make their own contribution to these systemic evils to be experienced by coming generations.[29]

Sometimes this "evil" can become embodied in particular persons and specific societies. One can trace a long line of persons/societies whose deeds we have thought to be so terrible that words like "sinful" and "bad" seem inadequate to describe them. Only the word "evil" seems right, or perhaps "depravity" or "perversity" (though there are certainly instances where we have resorted to the language of evil much too quickly).

In thinking about these forms of "evil" that take on a life of their own, we move toward biblical thinking about the demonic. In a few late Old Testament texts (e.g., 1 Chron. 21:1) and into the New Testament, there emerges something approaching a limited cosmic dualism (Satan). This reality is represented as a transpersonal power that stands temporally (not eternally) between God and world, opposing and subverting God's work. In terms of the development of such thinking, one may speak of anti-God forces, initially embodied in historical figures (e.g., the pharaoh), which in theological reflection over time are thrown onto a cosmic screen, taking on personalized "metaphysical" proportions (see Isa. 14; 30:7; Ezek. 28). Or in more objective terms, a buildup of historical evil over time becomes systemic, affecting even cosmic spheres.

God is linked to each of the above three types of suffering in varying ways, and how that linkage is made with respect to specific situations will shape pastoral directions to be taken. On the one hand, God creates a world with risks and challenges, wherein suffering is part of life apart from sin, but also a world wherein sin is possible and can intensify that suffering experience and bring still-further suffering in its train. On the other hand, God sustains a world wherein sin and its effects are carried along and over time are built more

29. For varying ways in which the Old Testament speaks of the perseverance and power of evil, see Jon Levenson, *Creation and the Persistence of Evil: The Jewish Drama of Divine Omnipotence* (San Francisco: Harper & Row, 1988).

116

deeply into the structures of existence. God does judge the world in and through the created moral order, acting within the interplay of human actions and their consequences, so that sin and evil do not go unchecked in the life of the creation. And finally, God will enter deeply into the sufferings of this world and use that very suffering to bring suffering to an end. To that topic I now turn.

Suffering as the Effect of a Vocational Choice

Not all suffering is vocational, as we have seen, but the vocation to which God's followers are called will often entail suffering. Indeed, suffering may become a vocation for us because it is a vocation for God. We might say that the divine vocation made especially evident in the cross enables a claim such as this: suffering is God's chief way of being powerful in the world. And that way of God is commended to each of God's followers, not for the sake of suffering in and of itself, some kind of masochistic move, but suffering that enters deeply into the lives of other people, especially those who are needy in some way. In that Immanuel-like move, our words and deeds have the potential to transform suffering situations into good. In the midst of a culture that seeks to avoid suffering at all costs, this move will not be easy to pursue. But we do have a God who calls us into a suffering vocation for the sake of others.

As I have suggested, this topic falls into two interrelated segments: human suffering and divine suffering. Generally speaking, human suffering as vocation can be appropriately discerned only if it is finally drawn into the orbit of divine suffering. And divine suffering finds its essential place only in relation to human suffering or, more broadly, the suffering of the world.

1. *Human vocation.* Suffering may be the effect of a vocation to which we have been called by God (see 1 Pet. 2:21, "Christ also suffered for you, leaving you an example, so

117

that you should follow in his steps"; see Mark 8:34). Or note the repeated language in texts such as 2 Corinthians 4:7–11: ". . . so that the life of Jesus may also be made visible in our bodies." Such vocational suffering, which is explicitly taken up for the sake of the neighbor and could be avoided, may be called the will of God (see Isa. 53:10; Luke 9:23–24). The phrase "could be avoided" is crucial in thinking about what Luke means by "take up their cross daily and follow me." Bearing the cross does not have reference to any kind of suffering or pain. Taking up the cross is a "daily" decision to enter into the suffering lives of others. We may not always suffer in taking up such responsibilities, but we often will. See the strong expectation of God that his followers will reach out to the needy neighbor in texts such as Deuteronomy 15:7–11 (see also the sharp words of Exod. 22:21–24). Such texts bring human responsibility to the forefront of the conversation; we cannot leave everything up to God because God has chosen not to do everything in the world all by God's self. What we do counts, for others and for God.

The Bible provides numerous examples of individuals who suffered because of their vocation. One thinks of Moses, who often suffered at the hands of his people in the wilderness, or Jeremiah, often called "the weeping prophet" (see Jer. 11:19; 15:15). Another example would be the Suffering Servant in Isaiah (see Isa. 42:1–4; 49:1–6; 50:4–11; 52:13–53:12). Scholars have not always agreed in their identification of the servant: an unknown prophet, the people of Israel, a faithful remnant, or all of these in some way. The suffering of the servant on behalf of others is explicitly stated to be God's will (53:4, 6, 10), and the servant willingly took the way of suffering and death for the sake of all the people (53:12). Though Christians often claim that these texts are most clearly seen in Jesus' life of suffering and death (see, e.g., Matt. 8:17; 16:21; Acts 8:32–33), we dare not assume that such an interpretation relieves the people of God, individually or as a whole, from their vocational responsibilities.

2. *Divine vocation.* The God who calls others to a vocation that may entail suffering is no stranger to that kind of vocation and to that suffering. The God who "knows" the sufferings of Israel (Exod. 3:7) has in Jesus Christ entered deeply into our suffering world and made it his own so that neither suffering nor evil constitutes a final word for the creation. God is not like a mechanic who chooses to fix the suffering of the world from outside the world; God is more like a good medicine, choosing to heal the world from within, by entering deeply into its life. God saves the world by taking its suffering into the very heart of the divine life, bearing it there, and then wearing it in the form of a cross. As the apostle Paul puts it, "My grace is sufficient for you, for power is made perfect in weakness" (2 Cor. 12:9).

At this point I take up briefly the issue of divine suffering. Here I simply assume God's capacity for suffering, indeed divine affectability: God can be affected by the suffering of the world. Yet God's suffering differs from human suffering in key respects. God is not incapacitated by suffering in finding a way into the future; God does not become bitter or callous. In suffering, God's saving will for the world never wavers, God's steadfast love endures forever, and God's faithfulness to promises made will not be compromised.

The notion of a crucified Messiah is commonly thought to be a distinctively Christian formulation. Yet the Old Testament witness is not often taken sufficiently into account. The Old Testament shows that God did not suffer for the first time in the Christ event, and even more, God did not suffer for the sins of the world for the first time on the cross. The New Testament witness to the finality and universality of Jesus' suffering and death is certainly an advance on Old Testament understandings, but it is an advance on an already-existing trajectory of reflection about a God who suffers. To see the face of God in a crucified man would not be a radical move for those steeped in Old Testament understandings of God. The kind of God whom the early Christians knew from their

Scriptures (the Old Testament) was a God who could know the experience of suffering. In opening up the divine self to the vulnerabilities of a close relationship, God experiences suffering because of what happens to the relationship. This could be named "God's Problem." God seeks to find a resolution, and that becomes possible only through divine suffering. We recognize an Immanuel theology: God has determined to enter into our suffering situation genuinely and deeply, most supremely in Jesus Christ. God thereby makes a new future possible in which, finally, there will be no more tears.

In conclusion, three aspects may be discerned:[30]

1. God suffers *because* the people have rejected God. God does not remain coolly unaffected by human infidelity. In such cases, God speaks in traditional lament language (Jer. 2–3; 8–9). Jesus' words over Jerusalem stand in this divine lament tradition (Matt. 23:37, "How often . . . ?"). God's response to human unfaithfulness is not simply formal or legal. Rather, God is "deeply" touched by what has happened to the relationship (Jer. 31:20). From another angle, God's judgment is accompanied by the divine grief; God's anger is regularly accompanied by God's tears (see Jer. 9:10–11, 17–19). God mediates judgment so that sin and evil do not go unchecked, yet God does so at great cost to the divine life.

2. God suffers *with* those who are suffering and enters into their suffering experiences. One of the images that the Bible uses for God is that of a mourner (Jer. 9:17–19). Such divine suffering-with is evident not only with respect to Israel, but also for non-Israelites (Jer. 48), indeed for creation as a whole (9:10). God is not indifferent to human suffering, nor does God respond with a detached objectivity. But rather than seek to overpower the suffering situation from without, God enters deeply into the suffering situation, healing it from within.

---

30. For detail on these dimensions of divine suffering, see Terence E. Fretheim, *The Suffering of God: An Old Testament Perspective* (Philadelphia: Fortress, 1984).

3. God suffers *for* others: suffering is a divine vocation. In the image of Isaiah 43:23–25, God assumes the burden of human sin. This divine carrying of the sins of the people issues immediately in the unilateral announcement of forgiveness "for my own sake" (43:25). God takes the brunt of human infidelity into the divine heart and bears it there (Hosea 11:8–9). God expends God's own life for the sake of the people's future (Isa. 42:14, "I will cry out like a woman in labor, I will gasp and pant"). God engages in such a giving of self that only one of the sharpest pains known to humankind can adequately portray what is involved for God in bringing a new creation into being.

For this kind of God, the cross is no stranger. Nor are the extraordinary sufferings and losses experienced in natural disasters.

5

God, Faith, and the
Practice of Prayer

In the anticipation of natural disasters or in their wake, human prayers often fill the room. These prayers are voiced by persons of faith certainly, but in such difficult times virtually everyone seems to be praying in some fashion. Such prayers vary considerably in form and content, from deep laments over what is happening to self or others, to petitions for God to "intervene" and deliver one from the actual or potential suffering, and intercessions on behalf of others, both known and unknown. What effect do such prayers have? Can they stop the disaster from occurring? Can prayers turn the direction of the disaster (such as a hurricane or tornado) away from the location of those who pray (or others of concern)? Might prayers have an impact on God in such a way that deliverance from disasters can be accomplished? Given the common understanding that such prayers have little or no effect on the happening of the disaster itself, prayers seem often to be concerned only about the effect on those who have already experienced the disaster or on those who respond to help.

How might the biblical understanding of prayer assist readers in their reflections on such issues? Here I will cast the following considerations of key biblical texts in more-popular terms.

I begin with a working understanding of prayer in the biblical tradition. Prayer is communication between believers and their God within a relationship of consequence.[1] In seeking to "unpack" this definition, I consider some general comments on prayer in American culture, continue with some notes on the importance of God images in our thinking about prayer, and then move to claims about the efficacy of prayer and analysis of key Old Testament texts.

Initially, I cite several biblical texts regarding prayer and make several passing comments as a way of orienting readers to the strong view of prayer and its effects in the Old Testament. These texts inform many of the more-general comments made about prayer in what follows.

Reference	Bible text	Comment
Exod. 32:9–14	The LORD said to Moses, "... Now let me alone, so that my wrath may burn hot against them. ..." But Moses implored the LORD his God, ... "Turn from your fierce wrath ... and do not bring disaster on your people. ..." And the LORD changed his mind about the disaster that he planned to bring on his people.	Note the impact that the prayer of Moses has upon God and the shape of the future of the people of Israel.

1. On prayer in the Old Testament, see Samuel E. Balentine, *Prayer in the Hebrew Bible: The Drama of Divine-Human Dialogue*, Overtures to Biblical Theology (Minneapolis: Fortress, 1993); Patrick D. Miller, *They Cried to the Lord: The Form and Theology of Biblical Prayer* (Minneapolis: Augsburg Fortress, 1994). It is not common for prayer to be a topic in books on Old Testament theology. In my estimation, there is far too little sustained theological reflection on such a widespread Israelite practice. There seems to be a remarkable degree of continuity in the understanding of prayer as one moves through the Old Testament. For my own earlier reflections on prayer in the Old Testament, see Terence E. Fretheim, "Prayer in the Old Testament: Creating Space in the World for God," in *A Primer on Prayer*, ed. Paul R. Sponheim (Philadelphia: Fortress, 1988), 51–62.

Reference	Bible text	Comment
Deut. 4:7	For what other great nation has a god so near to it as the LORD our God is whenever we call to him?	The people of Israel do not pray to a distant God, but one who is present and close.
Prov. 15:8	The prayer of the upright is his [the LORD's] delight.	The prayers of the people are not a matter of indifference to God. God is delighted when they pray.
Isa. 1:15	When you [the people of God] stretch out your hands, I [God] will hide my eyes from you; even though you make many prayers, I will not listen; your hands are full of blood.	Also see Isaiah 58:4–9. Certain factors in the relationship can lead God to respond to the prayers of God's people with a deaf ear.
Isa. 59:1–2	See, the LORD's hand is not too short to save, nor his ear too dull to hear. Rather, your iniquities have been barriers between you and your God, and your sins have hidden his face from you so that he does not hear [or: listen].	The people's relationship with God and their prayers can be adversely affected by their sins.
Isa. 62:6–7	You who remind the LORD, take no rest, and give him no rest until he establishes Jerusalem and makes it renowned throughout the earth.	Issues of perseverance in the practice of prayer are raised and related to temporal realities that are real for God's work in Israel's life.
Isa. 65:1–2	I [God] was ready to be sought out by those who did not ask, to be found by those who did not seek me. I said, "Here I am, here I am," to a nation that did not call on my name. I held out my hands all day long to a rebellious people.	God is genuinely affected by the absence of prayer; indeed, God holds out the divine hands to people (a typical prayer gesture in that culture) and pleads with them to pray. Indeed, God asks why no one answered when they were called (Isa. 50:2; 65:12; 66:4; Jer. 35:17). Such answering and responding are ongoing issues (see Isa. 58:9; 65:24).

Reference	Bible text	Comment
Jer. 26:19	Did [Hezekiah] not fear the LORD and entreat the favor of the LORD, and did not the LORD change his mind about the disaster that he had pronounced against them?	Observe the effect that prayers have upon God and God's way into the future.
Rom. 8:26	Likewise the Spirit helps us in our weakness; for we do not know how to pray as we ought, but that very Spirit intercedes with sighs too deep for words.	No one knows how to pray aright! God will evaluate prayers and use what God can use.

In a general reckoning, the Old Testament contains 97 prayer texts outside of the book of Psalms; 38 of these prayers are spoken by laypeople rather than kings, priests, or prophets (see 1 Sam. 1).[2] Not all human speech with/to God is represented in the Old Testament with the specific language of prayer (*palal, tephillah*). At times conversations between God and individuals are portrayed by using quite-general speaking references (e.g., "Moses said," Exod. 3:1–12). Some commonalities exist with respect to the literary form prayers take, as seen in form-critical studies of the Psalms in particular (e.g., laments). Prayer may be individual (Ps. 13) or corporate (Ps. 44); it may be silent or audible; and it may cover an amazing range of subjects. Few limits are suggested with respect to its practice (e.g., 1 Kings 18:27–29; cf. Hosea 7:14; Eccles. 5:2). Moreover, prayer is not something that is peculiar to the people of Israel. See, for example, the prayers of "outsiders" in Jonah 1:14 and 3:8–10, to which God responds. Prayers for enemies or non-Israelites are also attested (Ps. 109:4; Jer. 29:7).

Prayer and American Culture

In considering prayers in the Old Testament, it may be helpful to examine certain understandings of prayer in American

2. See Moshe Greenberg, *Biblical Prose Prayer: As a Window to the Popular Religion of Ancient Israel* (Berkeley: University of California Press, 1983; reprint, Eugene, OR: Wipf & Stock, 2008), 7.

culture. In my experience, prayer in this culture is often shaped by efficiency, time constraints, success, and especially individualism. Prayers tend to focus on petitionary matters, especially prayers that center on the pray-er or those close to the one who is praying. A consumer mentality is often in the air, where short-term perspectives prevail and immediate results are expected. The function of prayer seems often to be like Weight Watchers: we want discernible results, something that is measurable and quantifiable, and quickly.

With such views so prevalent, the effectiveness of prayer is often questioned, not least in the wake of communal disasters such as 9/11 or Hurricane Katrina. It was reported that many people on the planes that crashed into the World Trade Center (and elsewhere) or were trapped in buildings or were experiencing the hurricane were praying to God. The following questions were voiced in my hearing: Were their prayers not answered because they did not have enough faith or because their sincerity could be questioned? Was it God's will that these prayers for deliverance from disaster were not answered? Or was God's will successfully resisted by the hijackers? God saw the plans of the terrorists developing before any human being did; did God try to stop them yet not succeed? Is God really in control? Were those planes out of God's control? Are prayers effective only in certain limited situations, perhaps related to the internal life? Are prayers for protection from physical danger or deliverance from violence finally futile? How might biblical views about prayer enable a response to those who voice such questions about prayer?

In view of these and other questions, a kind of cynicism prevails in many sectors of mainline (at least) Christianity about certain understandings or practices of prayer, perhaps even an embarrassment. A letter in the *New York Times Magazine* voices an increasingly common view: "Claims of speaking with God or hearing from God are delusional, dishonest or both. Such claims are made by the same people who, when things go bad, say, 'It was God's will,' and when they go well, 'My prayers were answered.' Prayer? It's like a rocking chair; gives you something to do but doesn't get you anywhere!"[3]

Such a minimalist view of prayer is more common than we might think. And actual prayers are often evident only on the edges of the practice of faith, perhaps at moments of personal endangerment or family crisis. Even those who are faithful members of their religious communities are often not able to speak very well about what prayer is or practice it with any confidence. People of faith are so often content with rote or formalized prayers, with little spontaneity or discipline.

According to some observers, in the last generation or so many members of religious communities have been living between pieties. They are not able to embrace the piety of their parents or grandparents, but they are not yet comfortable with a practice of prayer that they can call their own. At one extreme, prayer seems concerned mainly to find self, to transform the self. At the other extreme, prayers are focused on an effort to escape from self or to deny self. Both perspectives are centered on a question such as this: what can prayer do for me? In view of such understandings, the practice of prayer often has a self-centered look about it.

Moreover, an inordinate concern with getting prayers "right" often prevails among people of faith. The words of the popular hymn "Lord, teach us how to pray aright"[4] has probably contributed to such an understanding, as have the polished prayers that often pervade the sanctuary. As if there is one right way to pray! Such an understanding is a hindrance to the practice of prayer on the part of many a believer. So, for example, many people are simply not comfortable with the prayers of lament that are so open in placing a life situ-

3. A letter from Charles Eikel, Madison, Wisconsin, in *New York Times Magazine*, November 14, 2004, http://query.nytimes.com/gst/fullpage.html?res=9804E 5DF113CF937A25752C1A9629C8B63.

4. James Montgomery, 1818.

ation before God and the community (see below). Roberta Bondi captures one dimension of biblical prayer that could be helpful on this point: "One of the things that derails prayer faster than anything is starting with some sort of noble idea of what it ought to be. I stress that prayer is a pretty ordinary, everyday kind of thing. Yes, it has its high moments, but a lot of prayer is just a matter of showing up."[5]

In response to the individualism so prevalent in our culture and commonly shaping the understanding of prayer, one of the most basic things I want to say about prayer in the Bible is that prayer is a means in and through which God gets things done in the world. God acts in the world in and through prayers (and other means). To put that point negatively, God accomplishes less if we don't pray. How biblical texts might enable us to fill out that understanding will shape our discussion below.

Prayer and Images of God

A fundamental issue relating to the practice and understanding of prayer has to do with the prevailing images of God. Abraham Heschel puts it this way: "The issue of prayer is not prayer; the issue of prayer is God."[6] How one thinks about prayer and how one practices prayer depends a great deal on one's view of the God to whom one prays. And even more, it is not enough to say that the pray-er believes in God; what matters, finally, is the *kind of God* in whom one believes. We can probably work back from pieties we observe, including the practices of prayer, and create a grid of the God images in which they are rooted. Or going the other way, we can observe the images of God and discern the types of piety likely to be practiced.

5. "Learning to Pray: An Interview with Roberta C. Bondi," *Christian Century*, March 20–27, 1996, 330.

6. Abraham Joshua Heschel, *Moral Grandeur and Spiritual Audacity: Essays Edited by Susannah Heschel* (New York: Farrar, Straus & Giroux, 1996), 107.

129

The images of God tend toward extremes in many quarters and often complicate the conversation about God and prayer. On the one hand, God may be the uninvolved overseer, sitting on the front porch of heaven and watching the world go by. In words of one believer, "God is an absentee landlord." When pressed, she replied, "Your calls are seldom returned, and nothing much gets done." On the other hand, God is absolute monarch, in total control of things, micromanaging the world. Yet as a student asked, "If God is in control, then given how unruly we all are, wouldn't we have to score God a crashing management failure?" The biblical materials tend to steer between those two extremes, for prayer makes little sense in either case. The wide variety of biblical images for God may help us chart some direction. One such biblical image that could inform prayer is that God is a seamstress or a weaver (Ps. 139:13), who weaves our prayers into God's quilting work in the world.

There is another way to depict extremes in our imaging of the God to whom we offer prayers: On the one hand, God is radically transcendent, so above and beyond the world that every prayer is a roaming cell-phone call that cuts in and out. On the other hand, God is buddy-buddy, taking no critical stance, speaking no prophetic word, and never being "in your face." This latter image of God accords with the popular song lyric: "Where seldom is heard a discouraging word, and the skies are not cloudy all day."[7]

Or on the one hand, God is superman/woman, who hears the prayers of those in trouble and, faster than a speeding bullet, is able to accomplish anything and everything. With such a God, no constraints or restraints of any kind are in view, and the only issue falls back on the sincerity or faithfulness of those who pray. On the other hand, often in reaction to interventionist talk (as if the only way God can

7. "My Western Home," by Brewster M. Higley, 1876; revised as "Home on the Range," by John A. Lomax, 1910.

act is to "intervene"), God may be present everywhere but never do much of anything, particularly in crisis situations. God is somewhat like the king or queen of England—with not much power, but showing a sympathetic presence and an ability now and again to sponsor some elegant liturgical occasions.

Such extremes in the imaging of God often skew the approach to biblical reflections regarding prayer. Thus biblical texts regarding prayer are often read in and through such understandings of God, and it becomes difficult to hear contrary voices from the texts.

Prayer and Relationship

Instead of these extreme images of God, I think that the root image for thinking about God in the Bible (and consequently thinking about prayer) is relatedness. In these terms, prayer may be considered an aspect of the gift of relationship that God has established with people, whereby God and human beings can meaningfully interact with one another.

Relationality is fundamental to thinking about the God of the Bible and the association of God and world.[8] First, relationality is basic to the very nature of God (evident already in Gen. 1:26–30, with humankind as "the image of God").[9] God is not in heaven alone but belongs to a divine community that is rich and complex. Hence, for those who are created in the image of this God, communal and relational understandings of the human should be primary. Second, God has established a genuine relationship with the creation and, more specifically, with the people of Israel. One of the ways in which this is evident in the Bible is the common use of relational metaphors (e.g., husband-wife; parent-child).

8. For more detail, see Terence E. Fretheim, *God and World in the Old Testament: A Relational Theology of Creation* (Nashville: Abingdon, 2005), 13–22.
9. See chap. 1, above.

Third, this relational God has created a world in which all creatures in all of their diversity are interrelated. The world is such that the words/actions of every creature reverberate out and affect the whole, shaking this spiderweb of a world in varying degrees of intensity and in positive and negative ways (see, e.g., Hosea 4:1–3). As they say in this world of Facebook and Twitter: "Connected, connected, connected!" Human beings have a greater capacity than other creatures to have these kinds of rippling effects.

The God of the Bible, by entering deeply into the life of such a world, commits the divine self to be involved in such interrelatedness in all of its complexities and open-endedness. God so relates to this world that every movement in the web affects God as well; God will become caught up in these interconnections and work within them and with them for the sake of all creatures. Hence, we need to place prayer within this kind of relational understanding of God and of the world. And issues of the efficacy of prayer (see below) are closely bound up with the complex character of this interrelatedness.[10]

Listen again to Roberta Bondi on prayer: "We are so verbal . . . that it's hard for us not to imagine prayer either as monologue, in which I tell God things and God listens, or as a conversation in which I tell God things and God answers back. But . . . *prayer is really an entire relationship*, and the verbal part is only one element. A lot of what we learn when we pray is to be quiet. We need to stop thinking that a relationship is constituted only by language. The closer we get to other people, and the better our friendships are, the more silence these relationships contain."[11]

How one thinks about the "relationship" with God is quite important. The language of relationship in thinking about God and the world is common in religious communities. But

10. Cf. chap. 2, above.
11. "Learning to Pray," 326, emphasis added.

if one were to "unpack" the sense of the word "relationship," what would it look like? What does it take for a relationship to be genuine, to have integrity, which is presumably the only kind of relationship God can have? The word "relationship," though commonly used, often has a rather weak meaning.

Among the important characteristics of a genuine God-human relationship is this: God so enters into relationships that God is not the only one who has something important to say. God knows that communication is a key to a healthy relationship. And so prayer is God's gift for the sake of meaningful interaction with human beings in relationship. Speaking and hearing, listening and responding—these are central to what it means to be in a relationship of integrity. Consider what would happen to any relationship of consequence if there was little or no communication between the parties involved.

The Bible does not speculate on how communications between God and human beings take place, but it does testify again and again to their reality. From the human side, the wide range of communication to God is remarkable: petition, intercession, lament, expostulation, confession, thanksgiving, praise, adoration—every form of speech imaginable seems to be drawn into prayers. But often someone asks, "How does God communicate in return?" Without going into detail, biblical texts suggest a remarkable range of ways in which God gets through to human beings: through words spoken by certain people (e.g., Moses); words in the night, perhaps through dreams; words spoken more directly into (e.g.) a prophet's mind, words that are suddenly right there. Or more subtly, an individual may not hear a word or think a thought, but has a feeling, perhaps of agitation, or a sense of something wrong or out of place. Or perhaps a feeling of peace or calm.

But God takes some risk in entering into this kind of communicating relationship. By giving us speaking privileges, God makes God's self vulnerable. For an example, we may

133

give God the silent treatment (see Isa. 65:1–2). The absence of such communication may be a sign that the relationship is less than fully healthy. Or people can speak words to God that hurt—words that reject or resist the word of God, presume upon the relationship, or disrupt the harmony of the relationship. Yet that is a risk that God is willing to take for the sake of the relationship. Recall Proverbs 15:8, "The prayer of the upright is his [the LORD's] delight." God is delighted when people pray, most basically because prayer is a sign of health in the relationship.

Another way to look at the issue of prayer is through the language of power. Prayer is a form of power given to us by God; as we have recognized, God is a power-sharing God—for the sake of a genuine relationship. Though God does not let go of any situation, God has chosen not to be the only one in the world with power, even from the beginning (see Gen. 1:28). Prayer is one way in which the power at our disposal can be more in tune with the will of God. Then God and human beings can act in concert with one another, rather than in competition.

In a nutshell, prayer is a means in and through which God can work on behalf of the divine purposes in the world. God can use our prayers to expand upon God's possibilities in a given situation. Prayer is not a substitute for action, but prayers and actions can work together (see 2 Kings 20:1–7). For example, no matter how open to God a given situation of illness may be, physicians and surgeons will still be needed. Prayer is that which brings the divine and human factors into the fullest possible power-sharing effectiveness. Prayer makes more room for God, giving God more space to do God's work. As Fernand Ménégoz says, "Israelite prayer tends to make the believer an energetic co-operator [with God] and not a beatified enjoyer of God."[12]

12. Via Edmond Jacob, *Theology of the Old Testament*, trans. Arthur W. Heathcote and Philip J. Allcock (New York: Harper, 1958), 176, quoting Fernand Ménégoz, *Le problème de la prière* (Strasbourg: Librairie Istra, 1925), 246.

God will be constant in relationship in a way that human beings can never be. God will be faithful to promises made, God will always will the best for God's people, and God's love will be there through thick and thin. God's core character will never change. Yet God will be deeply affected in view of what is happening to the relationship. God may be provoked to anger, may be disappointed and hurt, and may be absolutely delighted. And to our point, God will be affected by our prayers.

The Efficacy of Prayer

Some people speak with too much confidence regarding the efficacy of prayer. I pray for a parking place, and lo! one appears around the next corner. Or the efficacy of prayers is related to the depth of one's faith. If your faith is strong and sincere, your prayers will be answered. In response to such claims, questions like these have been asked: Do you suppose that Mary, the mother of Jesus, was praying for a nice place to stay in Bethlehem? Do you suppose that the apostle Paul did not have enough faith, and that was why his prayer to remove the thorn in his flesh failed? But among many other believers, even among those who hold the Bible dear, a remarkably limited sense regarding the efficacy of prayer is prevalent.

I suggest that the Bible speaks of four levels of efficacy regarding prayer. I cast them in more-contemporary terms. All too often, only the first item noted is considered seriously by persons of faith.

1. *Prayer has an effect on the one who prays.* Prayer enables fresh initiative, motivating the pray-er to redirect thought and life toward those persons or things for which we pray. Our sights are sharpened, our wills empowered, or healing takes place at some level within us. We may become more aware of the depth and breadth of what we have been given. Prayer transforms those who pray. For many believers, nothing more is claimed regarding the efficacy of prayer. Sometimes the

efficacy of prayer is even more restricted; it is nothing more than a meditation that centers us or quiets us down.

2. *Prayer has an effect on the relationship between the one who prays and God.* In and through prayer, the relationship with God is enhanced and made more mature. Yet if this level of efficacy is acknowledged, all too often change is thought to occur only on the human side of the relationship. People often think that God in relationship never changes in any respect. But the Bible claims that God is also affected by prayers offered.

3. *Prayer has an effect on God.* Much here depends on the image of God. It is often thought that God cannot be moved by any human words or deeds, and God certainly cannot be persuaded by anything human beings have to say. God will do what God will do regardless of what people have to say. Yet many biblical texts claim that prayers have an effect on God and contribute something to the way in which God relates to the world and to the shape of the future. Prayers of repentance make for rejoicing in heaven (Luke 15:7). Or, consider Psalm 22:3: God is "enthroned on the praises of Israel." God's rule is furthered or God's reputation is enhanced by our praising prayers. Even more, God is genuinely moved by our prayers, perhaps even persuaded by our prayers (see below). The Bible claims that prayer makes a difference to God and has an effect on what God accomplishes in the world.

4. *Prayer has an effect on persons or situations for which one is praying.* Somehow the power of God is made more available for a third-party situation because we have prayed (intercession). This is true whether or not that third party is aware of being prayed for. In this sense, prayer is a form of mission in and through which God accomplishes things in the world beyond the hearing range of our words or the doing range of our actions.

God and Prayer: Answers or Responses?

In thinking about prayer, believers often focus on "answers" to prayer. Indeed, they often look for *specific* answers (such as cure from a disease or deliverance from a natural disaster). If the Bible is any model, it is certainly appropriate to pray for specific matters, but it is often thought that if a specific result does not occur, the decision (and often the blame) lies with God, or the problem lies with the one praying (whether one's faith was sufficient or the prayers were spoken aright). The word "answer" often carries such a level of specificity that the pray-ers' horizons are sharply limited, and they often look for efficacy in the wrong places. Or sometimes prayer is so conceived that God's only options in response to prayers are "yes," "maybe," or "no." As Patrick Miller puts it (in a context devoted to a study of biblical laments): "The prayers do not assume that things are cut and dried, that God either answers prayer or does not. They seek to evoke a *response*, not just through the petitions themselves but [also] through all dimensions of the prayer. . . . Here clearly prayer is not simply 'Thy will be done.' "[13] Again and again in these prayers, the psalmist urges his/her own will upon God, articulating what God *should* do. The potential effect that this urging might have upon God introduces an open-endedness into the situation. God will take the human expression of concern with utmost seriousness, not least because God values the relationship and honors it. In view of such understandings, it might be helpful to speak of God's "responses" to prayers rather than "answers." When this language is used, it may occasion a greater openness to ways in which God is responding to prayers that do not look like specific answers.

More generally, I think the Bible would speak of God as the "subject" of the following actions relating to prayer: God encourages prayer, God receives prayer, God evaluates prayer, God transforms prayer, and God responds to prayer. God uses what God can use. A lot can happen in such a range

13. Patrick D. Miller, "Prayer as Persuasion," *Word & World* 13 (1993): 361, emphasis added.

of divine considerations. Pray-ers are called to release their prayers to God, not to hang on to them, and to let God work with them. Thus they may be better prepared for responses that may not look like answers!

Several Biblical Texts

Isaiah 65:1–2 (as well as Isa. 59:1–2) is worth another look. When the people of God do not pray, it affects God. People do have the power to make God less welcome in their lives, to give God less room in which to work; human action can narrow God's possibilities, not in a theoretical sense, but in specific situations in such a way that divine action may be genuinely hindered (59:1–2; see Ezek. 8:6; Zech. 7:8–14). The absence of communication may mean that God is not able to be the kind of God that God would like to be. This God remains eager for communication: "I held out my hands all day long to a rebellious people" (Isa. 65:2). On the other hand, prayer can provide more space for God to work in people's lives. God experiences "delight" when people pray (Prov. 15:8). It is a sign of health in the relationship when the communication lines are open between God and people. Prayer is a way in which the health of the relationship can be sustained.

Giving God the silent treatment may be compared with such interhuman mistreatment (by family or friends). Silence can shut others out and reduce the possibilities within the relationship for growth, healing, communication. Would this analogy work in the God-human relationship? Because of the God-given capacity for human resistance, and our amazing capacity to throw up roadblocks to protect our self-interests, God's possibilities for working in life may well vary from one situation to another. At the same time, God is a highly persevering God, unsurpassed in creating and finding openings in people's lives even when all the doors seem to be closed. One thinks of God's perseverance with the boy Samuel in 1 Samuel 3:1–10, in a time when "The word of the LORD was rare"; God keeps calling. But even then Samuel's response finally counts. Human prayer, even if it is no more than Samuel's "Speak, LORD, for your servant is listening" (3:9–10), may make a great deal of difference in a given situation. God is now more welcome, given more room to be at work.

Isaiah 1:15 likewise deserves a further look (see the similar theme in Isa. 58:4–9; Amos 5:21–24; Mic. 6:6–8). The lack of care for the poor and needy may narrow God's possible ways of working in human lives. The irony of these texts should not be lost. Personal communication with God is opened up by looking *beyond self* to the care of *the other*. An explicit connection is drawn between the way in which the disadvantaged are treated and God's reception of prayer.

Prayers of Lament

One of the most common types of prayers in the Old Testament is the lament. These psalms recognize that life is not all sweetness and light; indeed, life is often plagued by sin and evil, suffering and grief—and this for a multitude of reasons, from one's own sinfulness to abuse inflicted by others, to the experience of injustice in many different realms. Over one-third of the book of Psalms consists of laments. Several ways of distinguishing among laments have been suggested. One major distinction is between penitential psalms (e.g., Ps. 51) and psalms of the innocent sufferer (e.g., Ps. 13). An appropriate response to Psalm 51 would be forgiveness, and to Psalm 13, deliverance from whatever is causing the suffering.[14] I will focus here on the laments of the innocent sufferer, especially the individual laments.

14. Resources regarding the laments, Miller, *They Cried to the Lord*; Balentine, *Prayer in the Hebrew Bible*; Walter Brueggemann, "The Costly Loss of Lament," *Journal for the Study of the Old Testament* 36 (1986): 57–71.

Laments tend to follow a conventional form, with variations, which in turn helps reveal the flow of thought and illumine the situation of the one who is distressed.

1. *The address to God and cry for help (Pss. 13:1; 22:1).* The address to God is brief, without flattery ("O LORD"), and moves quickly to straight talk with God about the troubles through which the psalmist is moving.

2. *The complaint proper.* Telling it like it is (Pss. 55:12–14, 20–21; 102:3–11). There are various causes, from sickness and near-death experiences to external enemies and situations of injustice. Often genuine anger, even rage, emerges. All the hurts and distresses are not suffered patiently.

3. *The petition.* It is striking that an imperative is often addressed to God (an imperative!), appealing and indeed demanding that God address the suffering situation (Pss. 13:3; 22:19–20).

4. *Motivations.* Many different reasons are given for God to act on behalf of the pray-er:

- It is God's will to help the needy; I'm needy, so help! Be faithful to promises in view of an earlier history with God (Ps. 22:3–5).
- God, be reasonable: What good am I to you if I'm dead? (13:3).
- God, regard your reputation: What will the neighbors say? (13:4).
- I express trust (13:5a) and make protestation of (relative) innocence (17:3–5).
- Consider issues of fairness and justice (Jer. 12:1–4).

Hence, we need to ask: Why the remarkable range of reasons offered to God? Why give any reasons at all?

5. *A word from God (or God's representative).* This element is often not included in the psalm, but it is assumed (Pss. 12:5; 55:22).

140

6. *A resolution.* This commonly includes an expression of confidence that God will hear and act, plus a vow to praise God on the far side of deliverance (Ps. 13:5b–6; occasionally not present, as in Ps. 88).

This lament structure serves several important purposes for those who pray them (and those who read them):

1. It serves to channel the grief/pain, providing boundaries for it when the center no longer holds.

2. It provides an ordered way to work through times of suffering, from complaint to petition and finally to praise.

3. It names the enemy, puts the elephant out on the table, in the open, where it can more directly be worked with by oneself and others.

4. It provides language to speak when language fails, whether our own or that of a friend and caregiver. One should know the laments well enough to be able to use those that best fit a certain situation. Psalm 55, for example, is especially appropriate for certain abusive situations, but not just for any suffering situation.

5. It gives a sense of community in a time of isolation. Someone else has gone through hell; it's not just me.

6. It encourages a sense of genuine relationship with a God who is open to prayers of all sorts and is the kind of God from whom nothing need be held back.

Quotations from three scholars help round off this discussion. Walter Brueggemann helpfully observes that the absence of lament in the relationship with God "is finally a practice of denial, cover-up, and pretense, which sanctions social control. . . . Where there is lament, the believer is able to take initiative with God and to develop over against God the ego strength that is necessary for responsible faith."[15] The ego strength!

A close relationship exists between the voicing of laments to God and the voicing of laments with respect to institutions and their leaders. Again, Walter Brueggemann says:

15. Brueggemann, "Costly Loss of Lament," 61.

141

If justice questions are improper questions to God, they soon appear to be improper questions in public places, in schools, in hospitals, with the government, and eventually even in the courts. Justice questions disappear into civility and docility. The order of the day comes to seem absolute, beyond question, and we are left with only grim obedience and eventually despair. The point of access for serious change has been forfeited when the propriety of this speech form is denied.[16]

Marjorie Suchocki's comments are also insightful in thinking about laments:

Because prayer is to God, honesty is an essential element of prayer. Quite simply, if God knows me better than I know myself, what point is there [in] pretending I am other than I am before God? Prayer is not the place for pretended piety; prayer is the place for getting down to brass tacks. . . . Thus we might as well acknowledge our true state when we pray. We pray to God from where we are, not from where we consider we should be. And God, who knows us where we are, can lead us to where we can be.[17]

Patrick Miller, in speaking of the laments (especially in the book of Psalms), makes this strong claim and can sum up our discussion of this point: "The motivational dimension of these prayers [giving God reasons to act], therefore, is comprehensive and far-reaching. It pervades the prayers and suggests that one of the primary aims of the prayer for help is to *urge and reason with God*. . . . God may not be coerced, but God can be persuaded. . . . The mind and heart of God are vulnerable to the pleas *and the arguments* of human creatures."[18]

16. Ibid., 64.
17. Marjorie H. Suchocki, *In God's Presence: Theological Reflections on Prayer* (St. Louis: Chalice, 1996), 37–38.
18. Miller, "Prayer as Persuasion," 361. See Karl A. Kuhn, *Having Words with God: The Bible as Conversation* (Minneapolis: Fortress, 2008).

Prayers of Intercession

I have listed above a text that has to do with intercessory prayer (Jer. 26:19; for similar prayers, see Exod. 32:7–14; Num. 14:19–20; Joel 2:17–18). Note the impact that such prayers have on the lives of individuals and on the shape of their community. Prayer on behalf of others is effective. Sometimes we hear that prayer can have such an effect if those for whom we pray will know that we are praying for them, but in these texts that is not necessarily the case. These prayers make a difference with respect to the situation of a third party, and they have an effect not only regarding the people; they also make a difference for God. God's own future is changed in some ways because of the prayers of the intercessor. God will now do one thing rather than another that God has planned to do (see Jer. 22:1–5 and the "if, if not" formulation regarding the shape of the future for both people and God).

Exodus 32:7–14 will reward a closer look (for a parallel text, see Num. 14:13–20).[19] The people have sinned, and God speaks to Moses, announcing their judgment (through means that God does not announce). Moses implores God on their behalf, but he does not suggest that God's announcement of judgment is inappropriate. Nor does he make Israel's good deeds a part of his appeal. Moses' grounds are God's reasonableness in view of recent events, God's reputation among the nations of the world, and God's promises (Exod. 32:11–13).

What status do these reasons have for God? They do not somehow serve to attract God's attention; after all, it is God who has introduced the issue to which Moses' prayer responds. It is also clear that God is not being given some data of which God was previously unaware; what Moses has to say is not new information to God. The basic difference in the situation is that certain matters are being forcefully

19. For my earlier discussion of this text, see Terence E. Fretheim, *Exodus*, Interpretation (Louisville: John Knox, 1991), 283–87.

143

articulated by one with whom God has established a close relationship. Because God values the relationship with Moses, his prayer changes the decision-making situation from what it was before the prayer. Through such a prayer, the human party enters into the decision-making situation set into motion by God's announcement. Moses does not win an argument with God, but God so honors the relationship with him that God is open and willing to change directions. Human prayer can help to shape the future. The possibilities for the future are more open-ended. It does seem clear that, without the prayer of the intercessor, the results may well have been other than what they were.

Because of the way in which Moses has responded to God's announcement regarding the people of Israel, God now has some new ingredients with which to work. At least three new ingredients can be named: (1) Moses' *decision* to intercede on behalf of the sinful people. (2) Moses' *insight* into the nature of the situation; these matters are not new to God, but because Moses forcefully brings them into the conversation, they have a new status. If Moses thinks this way, that's important for God. (3) Moses' *energy*! If butterflies flapping their wings in Africa can affect the weather in Kansas, the new energy that Moses brings changes the dynamics of the situation with which God has to work.

And so Moses' prayer—which catches up his decision, insight, and energy, and had not been present before—is now placed at the service of God. God now has more possibilities with which to work because God honors what Moses brings into the decision-making moment (see Isa. 43:4 for God's honoring of the people). What believers have to say counts with God; what they say makes a difference in the situation.

Let us consider some words of caution. We must not forget that this is a genuine relationship between God and ourselves. Thus the relationship is not mechanical in nature, as if our prayers trigger in God some already-programmed responses. One must insist on the living, dynamic character of the relationship. Responses within any relationship—with other human beings or with God—are never programmed or predictable, even between those who indeed know each other well. And this is even more the case in that God is God and we are not.

Another factor that we need to take into account is the pervasiveness of sin, evil, and other factors (such as randomness) in life. These realities can disrupt God's responses to our prayers. For example, we pray for healing, and healing is not forthcoming. When that happens, we may end up blaming God for not answering our prayers or wondering why God did not answer our prayers. We so often make God the heavy in these matters. Yet it may have been the medicine we were taking or not taking; it may have been a member of the medical community whose skills were limited or who had too much to drink the night before; it may be that a lack of financial support for medical research on our part meant that a breakthrough in treating a particular disease was not there in time. Any number of other human failings could be cited. Sometimes when we pray, we may think, "All that is at work in a given situation is our prayer and God." But a multitude of other factors are commonly present in any such moment. Some of those factors may be so resistant to God's will that God's will is not done. And God's heart is the first heart to break; God's tears are the first to flow.

This may be a hard idea to grasp. Our understanding might be helped if we drew a large X on the board. The center of the X is every present moment. If we draw arrows from the left side of the X toward the center of the X, these arrows stand for all the factors that affect any given situation. They would include such things as prayers, God's will and action, the skill of the doctors, the condition of the patient, the helpfulness of family and friends, and the effectiveness of the medication. If we then draw arrows leading to the right of the X, leading away from the center of the X, these would

145

include what has occurred on the far side of the suffering situation. These realities might include God's using for good whatever has occurred.

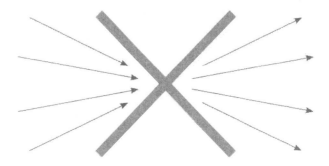

Just the complexity of the causes that feed into any moment in life prevent us from tracking in any precise way the connections between our prayers, God's responses to our prayers, and other factors that impinge on a given situation. We cannot reduce such situations to absolute clarity or think that God's ways may be discerned with precision. But something like this can be said: God may well be deeply involved in a suffering situation, and God's will for a positive resolution may be reasonably clear. Yet the accumulated effects of sinfulness and other factors at work in a given situation may be such that even God's options are limited in view of divine commitments made in the God-human relationship.

An analogy may be suggested: human sinfulness has occasioned numerous instances of the misuse of the environment. Some of that misuse (e.g., pesticides) has caused cancer in human beings and devastated animal populations. Human beings may be forgiven for their sin, but the effects of their sinfulness will continue to wreak havoc on those involved beyond the act of forgiveness. We confess that in response to prayer (and in other ways), God is at work in these devastating effects, struggling to bring about positive results in and through human (and other) agents. But one must also speak a

"Who knows?" (e.g., 2 Sam. 12:22; Joel 2:14) or a "Perhaps" (Jon. 3:9 GNT) with regard to the effect of that divine work upon specific persons and particular generations. It is not a question as to whether God wills good in the situation, but whether, given God's own self-limited ways of responding to evil and its effects in the world, what can actually be done and how and when.

To conclude, prayer is a God-given way for God's people to make a situation more open for God, to give God more room to work, knowing that God desires to be close to people. In all this, we are to recognize that God always has our best interests at heart. Prayers do shape the future in ways different from what would have been the case if no prayers had been uttered. At the same time, what human beings do (in addition to praying) has genuine efficacy, and consequently the shape of that future in differing situations will vary. And this is because of the kind of God with whom we have to do and the kind of relationship that God has established with us.

God honors that relationship. Given that reality, this God is not revealed as one who is unbending or unyielding, or one who assumes a take-it-or-leave-it attitude. The people of God are not in the hands of an iron fate or a predetermined order of things. God is open to taking new directions in view of new times and places; God is open to changing course in view of the interaction within the relationship, including prayers. Yet, never changing will be God's steadfast love for all, God's saving will for everyone, and God's faithfulness to promises made. God will keep promises.

The people of God have been gifted with the power of prayer as a means in and through which God accomplishes things in the world. Prayer is one way in which the mission of God can be furthered in the life of the world—even beyond the range of our voices. Even in the midst of natural disasters.

Conclusion

Understandings of natural disasters and God's role in them vary considerably, both within a given religious tradition (such as Christianity) and among different faith perspectives (as in Christianity and Islam). The Bible itself seems not to have a single approach to the issues such disasters present. The biblical writers certainly know of natural disasters and report on them with some regularity. At the same time, the way in which God is related to these events is not as crystal clear as many Bible readers would like to think. Some texts are thought to focus on issues of sin and judgment (e.g., the flood), and others on issues of the nature of the created order (Job). And how one might bring such understandings together is not altogether evident.

The way in which God is thought to be involved in natural disasters in our own time is heavily influenced by the way in which one reads these disaster texts in the Bible. Considerable continuity is often thought to exist between God's involvement in biblical times and God's involvement now. Others will speak more of discontinuity. Hence, understandings on the part of Bible readers with respect to how God continues to be involved in such disasters range widely, from divine absence to a particular intensity of presence. For example, God is said to make such disasters happen and to aim them at certain targets. We may not understand just how God is involved, but God, who is thought to be all-controlling, must have a reason for such disasters and precisely shapes the situation to bring them about. Others think that such disasters are unfathomable and that it is futile or just plain wrong to probe the "Why?" questions. For still others, if God is in any way involved in such disasters, it must mean that God is not good or loving—since suffering is not consistent with a good or loving God. We tend not to consider carefully that suffering is sometimes a good thing if it serves life. For still others, the issue boils down to divine power and the exercise or non-exercise thereof. And so, all too often, some may conclude that God does not exist or that God is a tyrant or that God is powerless. For still others, God *lets* these disasters happen (whether generally or specifically). Sorting out these possibilities in relation to key texts has been an issue for us in these chapters.

The Bible does not shy away from linking God to natural disasters, from the flood story onward. At the same time, how one speaks about that link has considerable import on the witness of the church to the God in whom we believe. And how God is to be related to the ongoing disasters that all of us have experienced has no little practical impact.

My analysis in chapter 1, regarding several key themes in the Genesis creation accounts, set the stage for such considerations. In Genesis 1–2, creation is understood not as a finished product or a static state of affairs but as a dynamic process in which the future is open to a number of possibilities and in which God's engagement with creaturely activity is crucial for creational developments. God's creation is intended to go somewhere; it is a work in progress. Built into the very structure of things is its potential of becoming something more or even something different. In the development of such a universe, God chooses to involve that which is other than God, from human beings to earthquakes, tsunamis, periodic extinction of species, volcanic eruptions, and storms galore. All of these "creatures" of God participate with God in the continuing creation of the universe. *An important point for me: natural disasters are a key agent of God in the continuing creation of the world.* How might this biblical perspective inform our consideration of natural disasters in our own time?

Choosing this way of creating the world will inevitably entail both human and animal suffering. In other words, human suffering may (indeed, is likely to) occur in our world because of the way in which God has chosen to create the world. The book of Job recognizes this connection. It explores various factors related to Job's suffering and will finally emerge with the viewpoint that his experience of suffering has to do with the nature of God's creation and the way in which it continues to be created. In effect, human suffering, even suffering such as Job's, may occur in a good, well-ordered, and reliable creation, because this world is not a risk-free world! In other words, one clear response as to why Job is suffering is that God's created order has significant chaotic elements that carry much potential danger to human health. *And* God has chosen not to manage this world to make sure that no one gets hurt by it. God will let the creatures be what they are created to be, and in their finitude, human beings will have to struggle to work with that reality.

God's directive to Job to "gird up" his loins (Job 38:3; 40:7) is a call for him (and for us) to probe his experience of suffering more deeply *in terms of the complexity of God's design of the creation and his own place within it.* God's questions to Job demonstrate that in order to understand his personal suffering, he must revise his evaluation of the nature of the creation and the way in which God has chosen to work in and through it. The becoming of creation contains risks for human beings.

At the same time, human behaviors have had an ongoing adverse impact on these developments in the life of the world. The story of the flood and other biblical stories of natural disasters (e.g., the plagues in Egypt) are examples of how human sin has intensified these negative developments in the created order. Not least because of the highly inter-related world in which we live, human sin has meant that both human lives and the life of other creatures have suffered in much more profound ways.

And so we draw several initial conclusions regarding God's participation in natural disasters. We cannot get God off the hook. This is the case from at least two perspectives. On the one hand, such natural disasters are an integral part of God's creational design: God created a world in which such disasters are integral to the becoming of the world quite apart from human behaviors. On the other hand, specific natural events may be made more severe by human sin, in connection with which one might—indeed, I would say, *must*—speak of divine judgment. In either case, God cannot be removed from some kind of complicity.

At the same time, God is involved in the healing of the environment, so that promises regarding the positive future of our world can be made: the wolf will dwell with the lamb, and waters shall break forth in the wilderness and streams in the desert (see Isa. 11:1–9; 35:1–10; 65:17–25). And not least because of significant environmental efforts in our own time, signs of such a positive future are manifest all along the way. Meanwhile we remember that though Jesus stilled a storm, he didn't remove all storms from the life of the world; though Jesus cured individuals of diseases, he didn't rid the world of those diseases. To use the Gospel of John's "sign" language, Jesus' actions point to a future world, thereby signaling that the kind of world Isaiah envisioned is on its way. Jesus provided signs of a different future that God has in store for the natural world. And God has enlisted the words and deeds of human beings in moving forward that future.

The world that God has created is in process, and one effect of that reality is that it is not a risk-free place for human beings or animals. There is much about God's creation, beautiful and wonder-filled as it is, that is potentially dangerous for human life and health. God has purposefully created it that way. And even though God has full knowledge of the world's harmful potential for its creatures, God did not provide danger-free zones for human beings, even for the righteous like Job. That kind of world, for all the suffering that may result, is deemed necessary for it to be a good world, one that is full of life and creativity.

Because we, like Job, are a part of this interconnected and disorderly world, we may, like Job, get in the way of its workings and get hurt. And we can certainly make things worse for ourselves—finitude again!—such as being insufficiently attuned to the workings of such a dynamic world. So we build homes on the slopes of Mount Saint Helens, or on insufficiently secured coastal areas and floodplains, or on the edge of earth faults. Moreover, human sin can intensify those suffering possibilities, even where no necessary relationship exists between such human suffering and human sin.

In sum, to say that the creation is good is not to say that it is perfect, as we have seen; at the same time, to say that God's creation is not perfect is not to say that moral evil makes it imperfect. For Job to understand his suffering, then, he needs to recognize that God has not created a world free from vulnerability. And God has chosen not to manage such a world to make sure that no one gets hurt; God will let the creatures be what they are created to be, with all of the potential for creaturely suffering. God has made this creational move for the sake of the fullest life possible. At the same time, and this point is important, Job's perspective and that of his friends must be allowed to be openly and thoroughly voiced before such a divine response can be fully appreciated.

On another level, it is not entirely clear why God created this kind of world. Several directions for thought have been suggested. It is often proposed that only a world of some disorder and uncertainty could be productive of genuine life.

Such a creation is necessary if the creation would be other than a drab, ever-the-same world. Such a lively and messy creation (to use our images from Gen. 1–2) is necessary if there is to be novelty, surprise, and ever-new creative ventures on the part of both God and creatures. And God will sustain such a world, which is both ordered and open-ended (and dangerous), because of its continuing *creative potential.* In the face of suffering, one might wish (with Job) that God would have created a different world or at least managed it differently. But the potential for suffering on the part of both human beings and animals is the cost of living in such a creative place.

The future is not fully settled. The moves that the people of God make in their lives matter to God and to creation because of the relationship God has established with them; in genuine relationships the decisions of *both* parties count. So God takes into account what people say and do in moving into the future. Think of God as a quilt maker. God takes the threads and the patches of our words and deeds and weaves them into the quilt of God's new heaven and new earth. What we do and say makes a difference in the shape that the future will take. Indeed, they make a difference in the *future of God* (see Jer. 22:4–5).

I am amazed at how often the language of fatalism creeps into our thinking about the future. It is commonly thought that it does not make any difference what we do about, say, justice or the environment, that God has the future all mapped out, and that what human beings do is ultimately irrelevant. But it should be made clear that the future is partly settled and partly unsettled. It is partly settled, yes: there will be a new heaven and a new earth. But the future is also unsettled: our words and deeds in our world will make a difference in the shape of creation's future.

Texts such as those we have considered in this study give significant responsibilities to human beings. We cannot sit back and assume that God will take care of everything or that the future of the creation is solely in God's hands. *Ultimately*, the creation is in God's hands, yes, but in the meantime, human beings are called not to passivity but to genuine engagement, and the decisions we make and actions we take will have significant implications for the future of this untamed creation and even for the nature of God's future.

What you do and say and pray counts!

155

Scripture Index

157

159

44:7–8 50n13
50:24–25 50n13

Lamentations

3:38 100n9
3:64–66 50n13
5:20 103

Ezekiel

7:27 50
8:6 138
22:31 50, 113
28 116
34:1–4 34

Hosea

4:1–3 5, 50n12, 54, 115, 132
6:4 49
7:14 126
8:7 53n22
10:13 50
10:13–15 49n11, 53n22
11:1–9 49
11:8–9 121
13:7–9 53n22
13:16 53n22

Joel

2:14 147
2:17–18 143

Amos

3:6 98n7, 100n9
4:1–3 49n11
5:21–24 139
7:1–6 97

Jonah

1:4 77
1:12 77

1:14 126
3:8–10 48, 126
3:9 147
4:2 48

Micah

6:6–8 139

Zechariah

1:15 56, 111
7:8–14 138

Old Testament Apocrypha

2 Maccabees

7:28 18n22

Wisdom of Solomon

11:17 20n26

New Testament

Matthew

5:45 51, 78n12, 87
8:17 118
16:21 118
23:37 120
24:37–39 45
26:36–40 107
27:46 103

Mark

8:34 117–18
15:34 103

Luke

9:23–24 118
15:7 136

John

1:14 23n34
3:8 20n25
9:1–3 14n11
9:2–3 98
9:3 98n6
9:3–4a 98n6

Acts

8:32–33 118
10:42 48

Romans

1:24 50
1:26 50
1:28 50
4:17 18n22
8:19–23 5
8:26 126
13:4 113

2 Corinthians

4:7–11 118
12:9 119

Galatians

6:7 50

Hebrews

5:7 107
11:3 18n22
11:7 45

1 Peter

2:21 117–18
3:20–21 45

2 Peter

2:5 45
3:5–10 45

Made in the USA
Columbia, SC
20 August 2020